"Bill Eddy has a well-deserved international reputation for his insights and training for professionals in dealing with high conflict adults. His newest book, *Mediating High Conflict Disputes,* underscores that reputation and adds his stature as a master trainer of mediators.

A focused lens on just one chapter of this breakthrough book helps us understand Eddy's brilliance and contribution to the mediation training field. I am particularly taken with the chapter on Pre-Mediation Coaching.

In my own training and writing, I have stressed the importance of starting mediations with PPP (Private Preliminary Planning Sessions) with each party. While this protocol differs from strategies by mediators who favor joint sessions with the parties only, I have found that the PPP helps build rapport with the mediator and the parties and prepares parties for a successful mediation through education and direct coaching.

Eddy's chapter takes the PPP to a new level of understanding and nuance. His insights and tips are applicable to the low and moderate parties as well as the 10-20% of high conflict individuals. Just some of Eddy's contributions include:

- Timing and structure of pre-mediation coaching to maximize its benefits
- An agenda for teaching parties how to succeed
- Insights about high conflict mediation participants stressing the importance of going over material at least twice due to their reactivity and having parties' sum up coaching lessons to sear in the tips for later use
- The importance of the mediator taking the lead to control coaching sessions to assure that high conflict parties have the opportunity to soak in the mediator's help
- Moving parties to a future preventive vision rather than stewing about past hurts and failures

This book and its lessons will now have a place in my trainings and those of other instructors in Mosten Guthrie Academy. I cannot imagine a professional mediator working with difficult parties before being trained in the Eddy method (named *New Ways for Mediation®* because of its focus on new skills) as exemplified in this book."

— FORREST (WOODY) MOSTEN is a mediator, collaborative lawyer, author and trainer. Chair of the International Task Force for Online Mediation Training Online Mediation Training Task Force Resource Center (**mediate.com**), Woody practices and trains internationally online. He can be reached at **www.MostenMediation.com** and **www.MostenGuthrie.com**

"Roger Fisher and William Ury suggested focusing on the problem, not the people. Bill Eddy and Michael Lomax fill in the gap when the person IS the problem. This is an enormous help to mediators. However, mediators may react to their approach with skepticism or alarm, because it is completely counter-intuitive.

I am a good example. I have been a confirmed Interests-Based Facilitative mediator for decades, and also a fan and admirer of Bill Eddy and his brilliance. Because his approach is so opposite to my general approach and values — and counter-intuitive — it has taken me a long time to adopt his approach even in the face of difficulty with a clearly High Conflict Person as a mediation client. Of course, once I tried his suggestions, I found they worked wonders. I am hooked.

Now Bill Eddy and Michael Lomax have written the guidebook, Mediating High Conflict Disputes, and it is extremely helpful. In addition to theory and understanding, in addition to the EAR and BIFF approaches, Bill and Michael have provided a step-by-step guide, including sequences, outlines, scripts and case examples. It is truly a masterpiece, one that will be dog-eared by use in many a mediator's office.

Thank you, Bill and Michael. It's a great addition to the High Conflict Institute library."

— ZENA ZUMETA, Esq., Mediator and Trainer,
Ann Arbor, Michigan

"A survival guide for anyone caught (personally or professionally) in the middle of a toxic conflict. Here are clear, concise tactics to help people who seem beyond help—and to save your own sanity."
— AMANDA RIPLEY, author of *High Conflict: Why We Get Trapped and How We Get Out*. New York Times best-selling author and journalist

"As a divorce attorney and mediator for more than 30 years, I have heard people say that it is impossible to mediate high conflict matters more times than I can count. With this book, Bill Eddy and Michael Lomax have upended that paradigm and have forever changed the face of mediation. This book is simply a MUST for every dispute resolution professional going forward and will be my go-to resource forevermore!"
— SUSAN GUTHRIE, Leading family law attorney, mediator and the award-winning host of *The Divorce & Beyond* Podcast

"It is great to see this practical and readable book that focuses on high conflict behaviors. This book will benefit all those involved in Alternative Dispute Resolution processes and the specific focus on mediation is timely and useful. The extensive, well-known and highly regarded work by Bill Eddy in relation to high conflict behaviors is well extended with an excellent collaboration with Michael Lomax."
— PROFESSOR TANIA SOURDIN, Dean and Head of School, University of Newcastle, Australia, Newcastle Law School

"As a civil litigation mediator of 15 years and a committed student and practitioner of the High Conflict Institute method of negotiating and mediating with high conflict people (HCPs), I know it's not enough to understand the HCP, we need tips and tools to effectively work with them. The challenge has always been "what do I do when interest-based analysis fails?" This book informs us. It is essential reading as it is the missing piece that takes us past *Getting to Yes* and gives us confidence that ***yes***, we can work with those people when *the issue is not the issue—the personality is the issue*."
— JOHN C. EDWARDS, J.D., mediator, West Coast Resolution Group, San Diego CA

"If I took all of the training, conferences, books and experience I have been exposed to and put them into an all-encompassing, organized, easy-to-read and practical resource I would have *Mediating High Conflict Disputes*. Bill and Michael have captured the essence of these disputes and how, as professionals, we can help clients work through them."
— Elizabeth A. Hyde, B.Ed., LL.B., LL.M., Acc. FM, FDRP PC
Mediator/Arbitrator/Parenting Coordinator/Trainer

"It is an honor for me to recommend this book, Bill Eddy and Michael Lomax and to thank them for their extraordinary generosity for sharing their experience with the rest of the world in order to enable other professionals to deal successfully with HCPs. This book is an important and significant breakthrough made possible by creative thinking that combines multiple perspectives, the best in the world of therapy and the best world of law into the work of the mediator, who does not shy away from the challenge involved in working with high conflict disputes. These tools will greatly contribute to the work of mediators around the world, thus helping to reduce the amount of high conflicts disputes, prevent escalation, minimize the cumulative social harm, and in the long run will make the world a safer and more peaceful place."
— Michal Fein, leading family lawyer and mediator,
social activist and author of *Inspiration, Structure and Default - A New Israeli Law Reduces Litigation in Family Conflicts by 45%*
Collaborative Rev. vol 18(2) (2019)

"I have adapted and applied the structured methods outlined in *Mediating High Conflict Disputes* and have found the tools to be highly effective for long-term systemic change in the educational arena."
— Dennis Doyle, PhD, education consultant;
retired school superintendent

MEDIATING HIGH CONFLICT DISPUTES

A Breakthrough Approach
with Tips and Tools
and the *New Ways for
Mediation*® Method

Bill Eddy, LCSW, ESQ.
Michael Lomax, JD

UNHOOKED BOOKS
Independent Publishers since 2011
an imprint of High Conflict Institute Press
Scottsdale, Arizona

Publisher's Note
This publication is designed to provide accurate and authoritative information about the subject matters covered. It is sold with the understanding that neither the authors nor publisher are rendering legal, mental health or other professional services, either directly or indirectly. If expert assistance, legal services or counseling is needed, the services of a competent professional should be sought. Neither the authors nor the publisher shall be liable or responsible for any loss or damage allegedly arising as a consequence of your use or application of any information or suggestions in this book.

Cover design by Julian León, The Missive
Interior Design by Jeffrey Fuller, Shelfish

ISBN (print): 978-1950057214
ISBN (ebook): 978-1950057573
Library of Congress Control Number: 2021937936

This Trademark List sets out an illustrative, non-exhaustive list of trademarks or service marks owned by or conveyed to High Conflict Institute, LLC, in the United States of America and/or Australia: High Conflict Institute®; HCI®; BIFF Response®; EAR Statement™; New Ways for Mediation™; New Ways for Work™; 4 Big Skills™.

Unhooked Media, 7701 E. Indian School Rd., Ste. F, Scottsdale, AZ 85251
www.unhookedmedia.com

Also by Bill Eddy

High Conflict People in Legal Disputes

5 Types of People Who Can Ruin Your Life

Calming Upset People with EAR

So, What's Your Proposal

Managing High Conflict People in Court

BIFF: Quick Responses to High Conflict People, Their Personal Attacks and Social Media Meltdowns

BIFF for Co-Parent Communication

BIFF at Work

Why We Elect Narcissists & Sociopaths—and How We Can Stop

Dating Radar

Hiring Radar

It's All Your Fault! 12 Tips for Managing People Who Blame Others for Everything

Don't Alienate the Kids! Raising Resilient Children While Avoiding High Conflict Divorce

Splitting: Protecting Yourself While Divorcing Someone with Borderline or Narcissistic Personality Disorder

It's All Your Fault at Work! Managing Narcissists and other High-Conflict People

The Future of Family Court

Splitting America

New Ways for Families in Separation and Divorce:
    Professional Guidebook
    Parent Workbook
    Collaborative Parent Workbook
    Decision Skills Class Instructor's Manual & Workbook
    Pre-Mediation Coaching Manual & Workbook
    Online Course Coaching Manual

New Ways for Work Coaching Manual & Workbook

New Ways for Life Instructor Guide & Youth Journal

*To Alice, whose encouragement, feedback, pep talks,
and sense of adventure for nearly forty years
have made all of this possible.*
—Bill

*To Tammy: Your creative and dynamic energy
has had an amazing influence on
my work and my life.*
—Michael

Contents

Foreword

Mediation has come a long way over the past several decades. As an alternative to litigation, it has found its own identity and has established its rightful place in an increasing field of alternative dispute resolution methodologies. As with the evolution of any rising movement, mediation has expanded into several mainstream models, from its origins of "Facilitative" through "Evaluative" and "Transformative" and into "Therapeutic" and "Strategic." As these theoretical movements were evolving, Bill Eddy found a unique niche, with his insight that there exists what he has coined "High Conflict People" (HCPs). In fact, he asserts that this group of people comprises 10% of our population and HCPs are present in every walk of life. As co-founder of the High Conflict Institute, Bill has actively promoted the special ways with which high conflict people need to be managed, whether in mediation or in ordinary relationships. His wide-ranging collection of published books on this topic has served as a seminal contribution to our growing knowledge of conflict and its resolution.

Bill Eddy's latest innovative book, *Mediating High Conflict Disputes: A Breakthrough Approach with Tips and Tools and the New Ways for Mediation Method,* written with co-author Michael Lomax, continues his legacy of detailing and further refining his concept of the High Conflict Person (HCP), a concept that has proved to be extremely useful to and well-received by both professional mediators and the general public. This book will be of enormous practical value to practicing mediators across a range of settings.

Bill's gifts of simplifying complex psychological (and relevant brain research) concepts that explain the HCP, and offering practical, scripted interventions for effectively managing and calming them down, are on full display in this book. Moreover, the successful methodology of his *New Ways* model is featured in this book to include its use not only in divorce mediation cases, but in workplace disputes, elder mediation, and large-group disputes, as well. In this book, Bill and Michael further offer a range of specific, useful tips, and ethical considerations for the mediator in these settings. Also, they provide a comprehensive outline of the *New Ways* methodology, along with role-plays, for the practitioner to use immediately upon the completion of reading this book—a generous offering, indeed.

As detailed in this book, dealing with HCPs in the context of mediation requires a different way of thinking. Whether there is just one HCP, or two or more in a particular context of dispute resolution, the practitioner needs to understand and appreciate the necessity of operating differently with them than when mediating with "reasonable" disputants. The authors present, in simple and clear language, how the architecture and functioning of the HCPs brain appear, according to current neurological research, to be different than the brains of more "reasonable" people, and, as a result, there are expected and predictable outcomes in their behavior. Knowing these links between brain and behavior can immensely help the practitioner in not falling down the rabbit hole of escalating conflict and predictable impasse. The authors, supportively and repeatedly, remind the reader that most of the unhelpful conflict that arises when dealing with HCPs is created by the HCP, not by the practitioner ("Remember, it's not *you*, it's *them!*"). Their tendency towards conflict merely reflects the unique wiring and presumed limitations of the brains of the HCPs. Trying to persuade the HCP to be more logical and reasonable falls on deaf ears; it is a matter of *can't* rather than *won't*. The authors give practical ways to maneuver around the limitations of the HCP so as to increase the practitioner's effectiveness in helping the disputants reach agreements—no matter the context of the dispute.

As the authors guide the mediator through high-conflict disputes, they present step-by-step details of the process, the order of issues to tackle, and the on-going mandate for maintaining client self-determination of the content while the mediator maintains very structured control of the process. Throughout the book, the authors give good details and plentiful examples of scripted statements, specifically designed to calm down the HCP effectively and preemptively from escalating.

Some of the suggestions presented for managing HCPs are counter-intuitive, or counter to regular mediation training. For example, the authors recommend having the *clients*, rather than the mediator, set the agenda. This helps to focus the HCP on tasks rather than emotions and helps rein in their tendencies to be emotionally reactive.

And, while conducting mediations with an HCP, the authors advise against using the traditional "interest-based negotiations," in which exploring the interests of the parties come before making proposals. These authors suggest the opposite order of these in mediating with an HCP; make proposals first, as part of the critical need to set structure up-front, then interests can be explored within that discussion, not before. This approach helps contain the HCP from getting caught up in negative emotions and hijacking the mediator's best efforts.

The authors of this book also suggest, in spite of the multitude of workshops available in the mediation marketplace on the "The Power of Apology," that the mediator *not* support or encourage clients to apologize to an HCP. They dub it "Apology Quicksand" and view the HCP's demand for an apology as "… a move to dominate or humiliate the other party, and to justify their own behavior…By seeking an apology, they can deny any responsibility whatsoever for the conflict, when it often is partly or mostly their own behavior that was a problem."

And, as a last example of counter-intuitive suggestions, the authors discourage using a Transformative Model of mediation in workplace settings when high conflict people are likely to be involved. (*Note: Transformative Mediation is the model used exclusively by the United States Postal Service.*) The authors point out that this model is based upon encouraging insight and self-reflection within the disputants, which they assert is not possible with HCPs, and that it would only further focus them on their negative emotions, which tends to escalate conflict.

In sum, this book is an important, detailed, and practical summary of the special modifications of approach needed by mediators when dealing with disputes that involve high conflict. Such disputes typically have at least one High Conflict Person, who can drive the dispute to impasse, unless the HCP and the dispute resolution process are managed differently than in the usual ways. Whether you are a beginning or a very seasoned mediator, this book will show you the *New Ways* to do it.

—Donald T. Saposnek, Ph.D.
Author of *Mediating Child Custody Disputes*
Co-Author of *Splitting America* and *The Child Support Solution*

Introduction
Why We Wrote this Book

We first met in 2009 when Michael invited Bill, as co-founder of the High Conflict Institute® (HCI®) based in San Diego, California, to deliver a training for the Collaborative Family Law Group in Victoria, British Columbia. We quickly realized we shared a mutual fascination with conflict resolution and people with high conflict personalities. We also both enjoyed training other professionals to be successful in dealing with them. Michael soon joined HCI as a speaker and trainer. As colleagues and friends, we have delivered many trainings and presentations together over the last 12 years and are excited to be collaborating on this book together.

We have both been mediators for a long time: Bill for 40 years and Michael for over 20 years. While Bill has always emphasized family disputes, Michael has often emphasized workplace disputes. However, over the years, we have both mediated family, workplace, business, community, public service, and legal disputes. And we have noticed some surprising trends in these mediations.

About Mediation

If you are unfamiliar with the fundamental concepts of mediation, or just getting trained in mediation, here is a brief introduction. Mediation is a structured process of making decisions on any topic, which is guided by a neutral mediator. The mediator helps the people involved in a dispute (commonly referred to as *the parties*) to go through a step-by-step process to identify their issues and various solutions to their dispute until they reach an agreement. The key fundamental characteristic of mediation is that the mediator does not determine the agreements of the parties—the parties make the big decisions with the mediator's neutral guidance.

If it is a formal legal dispute, the final agreement is usually written up, signed, and filed with the court where the dispute has been filed. If it's unrelated to a court case, the parties may either have a simple written agreement or a formal contract. In some cases, there may be no written agreement as the parties both understand their part in the solution going forward and trust each other to follow through.

Mediation is becoming the preferred method for resolving more and more disputes, because of the cost savings, the reduced animosity, the ability to keep discussions confidential, and the speed with which the conflict can be resolved. Also, with the coronavirus of 2020-2021, courts have closed or slowed down while mediation on virtual platforms has grown rapidly. It is much easier and quicker to get into mediation than into court. It is also much more flexible, confidential, and usually less costly.

Interest-Based Negotiations

Mediation provides an ideal setting for interest-based negotiations. This is the most commonly used style of negotiation today, based originally on the book *Getting to Yes: Negotiating Agreement Without Giving In* which was published in 1981. (Bill still has his original copy and still thinks it's great!) It upended the traditional bargaining method of taking positions (making demands) and making concessions (or not) in labor-management negotiations, international disputes, and legal cases.

Nowadays, people start their negotiations by exploring each other's interests in order to look for solutions that will sufficiently satisfy both parties. In other words, interests are helpful and positions are not. This approach also emphasizes separating the people from the problem. It makes so much sense.

We were each trained in interest-based negotiations and have provided trainings in this approach. However, as we got more and more difficult cases, we realized that these traditional interest-based methods were failing and that high conflict disputes needed their own quite different approach. The parties came in with positions and demands, and one or both could not see interests—their own or the other person's. They intensely thought in terms of "I'm right and the other party is wrong!" In many cases, we realized that a high conflict person *was* the problem. We realized that we needed to take a radically different approach with high conflict parties, as we will explain in detail throughout this book.

New Ways for Mediation

Over the past dozen years or so, we and our colleagues with High Conflict Institute have been applying a variety of techniques in our own high conflict mediations which seem to be more effective. We have taught them to mediators around the world in our trainings. All put together, these techniques have become a method which we call *New Ways for Mediation*. New *ways* means an emphasis on new skills and tasks for the clients, and a different structure and skills emphasis for the mediator.

However, mediators can use any of these techniques separately as tools in any mediation or conflict resolution setting. While they were designed for mediations with people with high conflict personalities, we were surprised to realize that they can be used with reasonable people as well. Therefore, we want to point out that mediators should see the tips and tools in this book as adding to your tool box, not taking anything away. You may decide to use none of them, or some of them, or all of them. We are offering you the *New Ways for Mediation* method and techniques as *tools not rules*.

About this Book

The first section describes why mediators need to make several paradigm shifts in their efforts to resolve high conflict disputes, otherwise they are much more likely to fail. The second section explains the structure and steps of our *new ways* method. The third section addresses a variety of different issues and settings for high conflict disputes, with several case examples of applying these skills. Lastly, our Appendices provide outlines, handouts and role-play exercises which can be used for practicing these tips and the new ways method.

The examples used throughout the book are either totally made up or disguised from real cases. There are more examples from divorce mediation because we have had more high conflict cases of this type and also because most people can easily relate to family disputes. The skills translate to any mediation case types. However, we also give other case examples, such as in the workplace, business, and group disputes.

The principles of working with high conflict people go with their personalities more than with any specific occupation or type of dispute. High conflict people are everywhere. We wrote this book to make it easier to mediate some of their increasingly common disputes.

—Bill Eddy and Michael Lomax

SECTION 1

What's Different About High Conflict Disputes?

CHAPTER 1

Understanding High Conflict Personalities

This book is written primarily for professional mediators and mediators in training, but it can also be used by anyone who finds himself or herself in the middle of other people's conflicts. While this is designed primarily for *high conflict* disputes, the simple tips and tools provided can be applied to any type of dispute. However, before attempting a mediation, one should receive sufficient mediation training.

Have you ever been in the middle of a mediation when suddenly one of the parties jumps up? "If that's what you're thinking, then I'm out of here!" And they gather their papers and storm out of the mediation room, permanently quitting the mediation?

Or have you had a mediation fall apart early on when the parties can't even agree on signing the Agreement to Mediate? Or can't even agree on the Agenda? Or have to fight over changing the Agenda in the middle of the process? Or respond to each other's suggestions by saying: "That's the stupidest idea I ever heard."

We have experienced all of these incidents, as well as cases with uncompromising parties, silent parties, yelling parties, cases with one very high conflict person, two, and even more high conflict people. We have often thought: "So, what do I do now?"

High Conflict

High conflict is a term that is becoming more frequently used in legal cases, family conflicts, workplace disputes and even political polarization. High conflict people unnecessarily increase or prolong conflicts, rather than making good efforts to manage or resolve them. It often means taking an adversarial approach to conflict resolution that could be handled in a cooperative manner. Essentially, high conflict means trying to turn a potentially *win-win* situation into a winner-take-all *win-lose* situation. High conflict people undermine efforts to find interest-based solutions to their disputes.

Let's take, for example, two friends. Most people would think of friends as seeking win-win, interest-based solutions to problems. In this example (familiar to many mediators from their training), both are interested in having an orange, but they only have one orange between them. A win-win approach (interest-based approach) would have each friend explain why they want the orange to see if both of their interests could be met. In this case, one friend wants it to make orange juice and the other wants to use the peel in making a cake. Obviously, this can be a win-win situation in which they both can get 100% of what they want.

But suppose that one of these friends demands that he or she gets the whole orange, because of being older, or richer, or smarter (in their own opinion), and refuses to consider any alternative. The other friend points out that they can both get everything they want. But the rigid friend gets more and more angry and demanding—arguing for their position: "No, I should get it. You are wrong and I am right!" That's win-lose.

Insisting on win-lose when a cooperative solution could be found is the essence of high conflict disputes. The one trying to *win* has possibly harmed their friendship but can't see how and/or doesn't care. The one faced with losing will either fight back harder (adding to an already high conflict situation), or give up and go away, resenting the unnecessary loss and possibly ending the friendship. In high conflict disputes, the conflict often persists and escalates, involving more and more people, more resources, and more emotional stress for all involved.

Most of our lives today we are in cooperative settings, such as families, the workplace and communities. When problems come up, we try to talk about them and find win-win solutions, so we don't harm our ongoing relationships. Even in competitive settings, we have laws and rules. We often shake hands after the competition is over, such as in a ball game, in business, and in legal disputes. We restrain ourselves from extreme adversarial behavior, get more done and have more satisfaction by taking a win-win approach. Even when we lose in one of these competitive settings, we still make efforts to preserve our relationships, because it is a friendly competition.

However, we are seeing more high conflict behavior in all areas of society today, including in legal and business disputes. There are more people repeatedly turning win-win situations into win-lose contests. They turn peace into war. They take an opportunity for friendly competition and turn it into a drive to dominate or destroy their opponents.

High Conflict Personalities

When this win-lose behavior becomes the primary way that a person acts with other people and in their relationships, we consider them to have a *high conflict personality*. People with such a personality tend to have a pattern of four characteristics which repeat and repeat in their lives in many situations:

1. Preoccupation with blaming others (their *targets of blame*)
2. All-or-nothing thinking and solutions
3. Unmanaged or intense emotions
4. Extreme behavior or threats

Because of this, they frequently get stuck in conflicts that most people could easily resolve. That's why in high conflict situations we like to say: "The issue's not the issue, the personality is the issue." Most high conflict situations have at least one high conflict person and sometimes two or more.

High conflict people exist in all cultures and geographic regions. They can be very smart or very not smart. They can be poor, middle income or even very high income. They can be found in every occupation, although some occupations encourage or tolerate more adversarial behavior than others. They are often attracted to volunteer organizations, church groups, political parties and other groups that welcome everyone and are often unprepared for such difficult behavior.

At our trainings we often ask for a raise of hands to find out if people are seeing an increase in high conflict people over the past few years in their cases. Most people say "Yes." Some put up both hands!

HCPs

Throughout this book we will often refer to the abbreviated term HCPs, to mean *high conflict people* or *people with high conflict personalities*. This is not a diagnosis, but a shortened term for people with this intense pattern of conflict behavior. We understand that this term does not describe a full person, just as the term *alcoholic* or *diabetic* or *Californian* or *Texan* does not describe a whole person. It is not meant in any way to be judgmental, but rather practical in recognizing a pattern of behavior that needs a different type of approach by mediators and other professionals. The goal is to change our own behavior toward them, rather than to try to change them.

It is also important not to label any specific person as an HCP. Labels trigger defensiveness in all of us, whether or not they are accurate. The purpose of describing HCPs and methods for working more effectively with them is to adapt what we do and not to publicly embarrass them or isolate them.

Targets of Blame

HCPs are preoccupied with blaming others and not looking at their own part in a problem. Their targets of blame tend to be:

1) *intimate others:* those emotionally close to themselves, such as spouses, parents, children, boyfriends, girlfriends, close co-workers, close neighbors, helping professionals (doctors, lawyers, clergy); and/or

2) *people in positions of authority:* such as supervisors, business owners, police, government officials, government agencies, school administrators, doctors, lawyers, and so forth.

Once they have fixated on such a target of blame, an HCP may attack that person as the cause of all their problems or at least the cause of one major problem in their life. They may be willing to spend months or years and involve many other people in their efforts to get their target to do something, give them something, go away; or to even destroy their reputation, their relationships, their property or even their lives.

Such behavior may lead to trouble at work, in their community or with law enforcement. They may bring frivolous lawsuits as plaintiffs against their targets of blame, or have lawsuits or even criminal prosecution brought against themselves as defendants because they engaged in extreme behavior (usually aimed at their targets of blame).

We estimate from our experience in a wide variety of settings that approximately ten percent of adults have a high conflict personality. It may not be obvious, especially at the start of a relationship, but their extreme behavior eventually comes out over time or in a crisis.

Personality Disorders

People with high conflict personalities often have personality disorders, which is a mental health diagnosis. We are not teaching you how to diagnose a personality disorder. Diagnosing personality disorders is a complex task reserved for licensed mental health professionals who are providing counseling or other psychological services. We want to briefly explain personality disorders to help you have a general background understanding in order to know *what to expect* from them, *what not to expect* from them, *what not to do,* as well as *what to do* in working with high conflict people.

Personality disorders are an *enduring pattern* of behavior that is inflexible and exists in many settings in the life of the person who has the disorder.[1] This causes the person to have:

1. **Interpersonal impairment**, meaning problems in social relations in a variety of settings. They have a long-standing pattern of such problems as an adult, which may have started as a child and may last a lifetime, although the severity of difficulty may increase or decrease slightly with time. They often have few real friends and rely heavily on family members and others to solve their problems, such as lawyers, mediators, and government agencies.

2. **Lack self-awareness**, meaning that they do not reflect on their own social behavior. They tend to see all problems as caused by something or someone outside of themselves. They can't (yes, can't!) see their own part in adding to or creating their own problems and conflicts. Therefore, they generally feel like victims in

life and spend a lot of time feeling frustrated, helpless, vulnerable, afraid and angry.

3. **Lack of change**, meaning that they are stuck in behaving the same way over and over again (remember, they have an *enduring pattern*), even when there are negative consequences over and over again. In this regard, they are like alcoholics in denial. Except that people with personality disorders are even harder to change than alcoholics. They don't seek treatment because they don't think they have a problem. They think all their problems are caused outside themselves.

4. **Externalizing responsibility**, meaning they blame forces outside themselves when things go wrong. This could be some vague force which they feel is out to get them, such as bad luck, the universe, the government, or the weather. Or this could be a person or group—a specific *target of blame* (TOB). They truly believe this TOB is the cause of their distress, so that they are willing to engage in intense conflict with this TOB to relieve their distress.

Based on Bill's four decades of experience as a mental health professional, mediator, and lawyer, he believes that about half of those with personality disorders do not focus on a target of blame and therefore don't become high conflict people. Likewise, not all people with high conflict personalities appear to have personality disorders, but they do seem to have some traits of personality disorders. This causes them to have targets of blame, but perhaps with some limited self-awareness and some ability to change.

Diagram 1 gives an idea of the overlap of personality disorders with high conflict personalities, which helps you understand why they can be so difficult and resistant to changing their impaired behavior in a conflict.

Compassion for People with Personality Disorders

It is very important to have compassion for people with personality disorders and high conflict personalities. Personalities develop in childhood as a result of heredity, early childhood experiences, and the behavior modeled by the larger culture the child grows up in—none of which a child has control over.

Personality Disorders
Enduring Pattern of Social Impairment
Lack of self-awareness
Rarely or never changes behavior
Externalizing responsibility

HCPs
Preoccupied with Target(s) of Blame
All-or-nothing thinking
Unmanaged emotions
Extreme behavior or threats

Diagram 1

Of course, as adults, people are responsible for their own behavior. But if they don't reflect on their own behavior or make efforts to change it, they are unlikely to take responsibility and more likely to end up on repeated conflicts and often in disputes needing resolution with the assistance of others, such as mediators. Because of their lack of social self-awareness and lack of change, working with people with personality disorders or traits requires different strategies and skills, but can be successful if you understand more about them.

Conclusion

High conflict people (HCPs) get stuck in a pattern of blaming others (their targets of blame), all-or-nothing thinking, unmanaged emotions, and extreme behavior or threats. They have a narrow range of repetitive behavior that tends to maintain or increase conflicts. They may be approximately ten percent of the adult population. There is a wide range of how difficult they are, and they vary depending on the situation and level of stress.

HCPs overlap with people with personality disorders. We do not go into depth about personality disorders in this book (see our other books). The key characteristics to understand are that they have interpersonal dysfunction, they lack self-awareness of their interpersonal behavior, they rarely or never change their behavior, and they believe that their problems are caused by forces outside themselves.

17

Yet people with these characteristics can often resolve their disputes with proper knowledge, skill and a structured process which is very simple.

CHAPTER 2

The High Conflict Brain

Very briefly, we will discuss a bit about the brain, because it helps explain why high conflict people (HCPs) respond differently to conflict and how to help them shift from blame to problem solving. We are not neuroscientists, so this is a very elementary approach to help you understand where to focus your attention and where to focus the parties' attention.

Logical Brain, Relationship Brain

We generally have two different systems of conflict resolution in our brains. One, associated more with the left hemisphere, which we will call the Logical Brain. The other, associated more with the right hemisphere, which we will call the Relationship Brain. Here's a brief comparison of these two different approaches, based on *our interpretation* of the work of several neuroscientists, including Daniel Seigel in his books on interpersonal neurobiology and Allan Schore in his book *Right Brain Psychotherapy*[2]:

Generally, brain scientists have studied where the brain activity is when doing different types of tasks by looking at pictures of the blood flow. However, during most activities, there is some blood flow in regions of both hemispheres. It's just that one hemisphere appears dominant depending on the type of task. In general, they suggest that the left brain is dominant most of the time for adults when they are engaged in problem-solving tasks, although the right hemisphere is engaged to some extent.

However, in a crisis or totally new situation, the right brain apparently becomes dominant.[3] In extremely stressful situations, such as a traumatic experience, it appears that the right brain has all of the blood flow and that the left brain is essentially off-line. This way a person can put all of their energy into life-saving action (fight, flight, freeze), rather than wasting any time carefully analyzing which way to respond.

In other words, the right brain can be faster, but not as smart in a crisis. In a life-threatening situation, jumping to conclusions may make a lot of sense for fast action. But when you're solving a complex problem or resolving a dispute between two or more parties, you will want to use the analytical abilities of your left brain. If you're calm, you can use the abilities of both hemispheres, keeping in mind that the right brain also tends to be more creative and intuitive. The best decisions and solutions to problems tend to use the benefit of both hemispheres.

The corpus callosum is another aspect of the brain that seems to play a role in conflict resolution. The corpus callosum is the bridge of neurons between the hemispheres. Studies by researchers such as Martin Teicher and colleagues at Harvard University have shown that the corpus callosum is smaller in repeatedly abused children and some people with personality disorders.[4] This means that its harder for them to manage their upset emotions and get back to problem-solving when they perceive a crisis. They may spend a lot more time in defensive mode rather than problem solving. Many high conflict people seem to be on the edge of exploding or running out of the room when discussing their conflicts, and this may help explain why.

Also, each hemisphere has an amygdala (yes, we have two of them), which is the fastest part of the brain at sensing danger.[5] The right hemisphere's amygdala is reportedly larger in some people with personality disorders, so that they tend to interpret situations as more dangerous than the average person. Since this is physiologically based, it's important to understand that some people just can't suddenly calm themselves and may truly believe that an option that has been raised in mediation could feel life-threatening to them. In this book we will give you some techniques for taking this into account and helping people calm themselves in a conflict.

Mirror Neurons

Mirror neurons are another aspect of the brain which seems to play a big part in our relationships and in dealing with conflict. Apparently, when we see other people doing an activity, some neurons in our brains start picturing us doing the same activity.[6] Have you ever been in a meeting where one person crossed their arms, and then another person did the same thing moments later? Or crossed their legs, and then another person did the same thing, or maybe even three or four people? We don't always do what we see, but it seems that it goes into our brains as another way of doing things possibly in the future.

Emotions may also be influenced by mirror neurons, so that when you see a frightened or angry face, your face may feel like mirroring the other person's expression or behavior. And your facial expression can influence how you feel inside. "I feel your pain," is a common expression when we listen closely to someone, which may actually become true. Likewise, a happy face may also be mirrored, so that when you tell someone you just accomplished something or had a happy experience, they may start to mirror your positive expression. "I feel your joy!" they may say, as they may actually feel happier inside.

Some suggest that empathy is in many ways the result of mirror neurons. There is even some research showing that most people will mirror a baby yawning by yawning themselves—it's a natural empathy response. However, there is also research showing that those with antisocial personality disorder don't have this response for some reason, perhaps because they lack empathy overall. (But don't count on this as a test for finding people with antisocial personalities in your life.)

What this means is that we will be tempted to mirror the behavior of our high conflict clients, and many unwary professionals do. We have seen other people start to imitate an angry client, and then several people suddenly become angry. This appears to be how mobs operate, because emotions can be contagious. Fear and anger are contagious, especially in high conflict cases, since HCPs express a lot of fear and anger. But positive feelings can also be contagious. Therefore, try to stay calm in the face of their fear and anger, and your calmness will often be contagious to influence them to calm down.

Polyvagal Theory

The vagus nerve in the brain is the one with the most neurons branching out to our eyes, ears, face, neck, chest and abdomen, constantly picking up information.[7] Polyvagal theory suggests that this nerve also exerts control over the heart, lungs and digestive tract, and can trigger fight or flight responses, as well as shut down bodily functions in response to stress.[8] This may help explain why we have a freeze response in some situations. Polyvagal theory emphasizes the importance of a sense of safety in order to turn off our defensive strategies to allow positive social engagement to occur.[9]

Other Mental Disorders

While we focus on personality disorders and methods for working with high conflict personalities in this book, there are several other mental disorders with some similar patterns of dysfunctional interpersonal behavior at times. People with bipolar disorder, depression, high anxiety, addictions, schizophrenia, trauma history, ADHD, autism spectrum, brain injuries, and other disorders can usually benefit from the same tips and method we are going to provide in this book. No diagnosis is necessary to apply these skills; they are safe for anyone.

The High Conflict Brain

We all have a high conflict brain to some extent. It helps us survive in life-threatening circumstances. But as we have learned, there are some possible structural differences in the brains of high conflict people that emphasize defensiveness when logical problem-solving is really the task at hand. Mostly, the high conflict brain seems to be an ordinary brain that easily becomes stuck in defensiveness and has a hard time calming down, perhaps because of a damaged and smaller corpus callosum and larger right amygdala. Furthermore, we have learned that emotions are contagious for all human beings because of the amygdala and mirror neurons, and that high conflict emotions are highly contagious! So, we really need to manage our own emotions so that we don't also shift into our own high conflict brain when we could have solved problems.

People with high conflict personalities seem to be on the edge of high conflict emotions and behavior much of the time. When they shift into high conflict gear, it takes them a long time to calm down and return to problem-solving. Mediators (and all of those around these conflicts) often get emotionally hooked by these high conflict emotions as well and may contribute to the escalation. Yet we have the ability to intervene and intervene successfully in most of their cases.

We can do our best to calm their high conflict brain and work with their logical problem-solving brain by managing ourselves and following a structured process.

Conclusion

All put together, what we have learned about brain science can be applied directly to how we engage with our high conflict clients in mediation. We can work with their Logical Brain or their High Conflict Brain (the defensive parts). Given that HCPs and people with mental disorders tend to have heightened defensiveness, learning how to navigate around their defensiveness is a major task for mediators.

The challenge for a mediator is to help keep the parties calm enough to find the best solutions. Since emotions are contagious, a mediator who can remain calm in a conflict may be able to get the parties to mirror his or her facial expression and calm words so that they can focus their attention on finding solutions.

This interpersonal brain knowledge has helped us develop our new set of tools for high conflict mediation which are often the opposite of what we have done for years in ordinary mediations. You will discover that there are several surprising paradigm shifts in this new approach that your brain will probably resist at first. That's okay. Use the tools that work for you. The secret to managing high conflict disputes is in managing your own anxiety.

CHAPTER 3

The Four Fuhgeddaboudits (What NOT to Do)

While its generally best to teach people what *to do* when teaching a skill, in the case of high conflict mediation there are also four things especially *not to do!* We want you to know these and absorb them before we tell you what to do. We call these the Four Forgeddaboudits:

1. FUHGEDDABOUD trying to give the parties insights into their own behavior.

High conflict people are stuck in a self-defeating pattern of blame and denial that prevents them from seeing their part in their problems and conflicts. They are preoccupied with blaming others and avoiding responsibility. You cannot break through this, because it has become a part of their personalities for most of their lives. You could yell at them, say it softly, deliver a brilliant analysis of their self-defeating behavior or take a sledge-hammer approach, yet you will still not succeed at giving them insight into themselves.

Yes, this is sad to say, but it just means that we need to adapt our approach to dealing with them without trying to give them this insight, because if you do:

1) They won't get it and will instead become highly defensive about their own behavior.

2) It will harm your relationship with them because they will interpret your effort to give them insight as a personal attack, meaning that you don't like or respect them as they are.

Instead, what we do with *New Ways for Mediation* is to focus them on WHAT TO DO, rather than what not to do. We focus on new skills to use in the mediation process, rather than insight about ineffective behavior. We don't explore their interests, because that would involve insight into themselves and insight into the other party or parties, and that usually blows up into the attack-defend cycle we are trying to avoid.

This will save you a lot of time and stress. When you wonder "How can I make her see her part in this problem?" That's a fuhgeddaboudit! When you wonder "How can I make him understand what he's doing wrong?" That's a fuhgeddaboudit. Not only will you be unable to persuade them to think differently; your efforts will strain your relationship with them because HCPs interpret all feedback as negative feedback, no matter how constructive you mean it to be.

2. FUHGEDDABOUD emphasizing the past. Focus on the future.

High conflict people are stuck in the past, defending their past behavior as justified and attacking the *very bad* behavior of others. They are preoccupied with talking about how badly people have treated them and their efforts to recruit negative advocates to agree with them and help them attack those bad people (who are often those closest to them or used to be). The more they talk about the past, the deeper they get into their belief that it is all other people's fault and they have to fight for themselves.

The problem here appears to be that HCPs don't go through the stages of the normal grieving and healing process that enables most people to move forward in their lives, even after devastating losses. The most well-known stages of this process are:

1) **Denial** ("I don't believe this is happening to me");

2) **Anger** ("If this is happening, I'm mad as heck and I'm going to fight this every inch of the way");

3) **Bargaining** ("What if I change my behavior now," when it's too late to bargain against the inevitable loss.);

4) **Depression** (Turning inward and feeling the pain of the loss.)

5) **Acceptance**. But HCPs become preoccupied with anger and don't seem to go through the other stages, and rarely or never reach the acceptance stage.

The result is that they seem to be walking around with a lot of unresolved grief, which seems to overwhelm them when they look at the past. Instead, they become preoccupied with trying to re-write the past by defending and justifying their own behavior, and attacking and criticizing others. They never *get over it*.

This means it's better to steer clear of the past as much as possible. Instead, we focus on the future and looking at choices, proposals and information about *what to do* in the future to resolve or manage their dispute. Instead of asking probing questions about the past efforts or arrangements, we offer them alternatives or options for what they could do in the future. This may involve educating them about what others have done, usually telling about several scenarios so that they don't get stuck on attacking or defending one approach that the mediator has mentioned.

Of course, they may need to talk about the past some because it is often a past behavior that has brought them into mediation, especially the mediation of a legal dispute. However, put more emphasis on the future and what to do now. That's why the fuhgeddaboudit is *not focusing* on the past, rather than *never* talking about the past.

3. FUHGEDDABOUD emotional confrontations or opening up emotions.

High conflict people chronically feel helpless, vulnerable, weak, and like a victim-in-life. This appears to be because they don't change their own behavior to make things better for themselves, and because they don't go through the normal grieving and healing process. Focusing their attention on how they feel tends to make them feel worse, not better. They can't get it off their chests, so they tend to wallow in it.

Most people can talk about an upsetting problem for a few minutes to an attentive person and then feel better. However, HCPs instead get stuck talking and venting about how upset they are, over and over and over again, without getting relief. What we have learned (the hard way) is that it is better to acknowledge how they feel and then shift the focus onto a task. Then, they generally feel better when they're engaged in the task than when they are focusing on how badly they feel.

This means that it's very important not to confront them with anger, because that just puts them in touch with all of their own unresolved anger. And they can do anger better than you can! It also means that you shouldn't tell them that they are frustrating or difficult to work with.

In addition, this means that you shouldn't even ask them how they are feeling. Instead, focus on what they are doing or thinking about a proposal. If you want to make small talk before you get started or at the end of a mediation session, talk about a subject like the weather, traffic or plans for the weekend. An open-ended "how are you feeling today" can easily run into trouble, as it opens up looking at how helpless, vulnerable, weak and like a victim-in-life they feel.

In a high conflict divorce mediation in person, both parties were very difficult and they both had lawyers present who were familiar to the mediator and very helpful. At the end of two hours (the usual session length), the mediator acknowledged the parties' progress (even though it was small) and a second session (out of approximately four sessions) was scheduled, coordinating all five calendars.

As everyone was packing up, the husband's lawyer turned to him and said: "Don't you feel better now?" The husband responded loudly: "Absolutely not! [Pause] In fact, this was a total waste of time! [Pause] In fact, I'm never coming back!" And he never did.

What went wrong here? His lawyer put him in touch with his feelings, which were predictably negative, probably feeling like a victim-in-life. He immediately went into anger mode with its all-or-nothing thinking (waste of time) and extreme behavior (impulsively canceling the mediation), after two hours of a carefully managed mediation designed to help the parties stay calm.

Moral of the story? Don't ask HCPs about how they are feeling. Instead, focus them on tasks and ask what they think (not what they feel) about proposals.

4. FUHGEDDABOUD telling them they have a high conflict personality.

Out of frustration, professionals occasionally tell their clients that they have high conflict personalities or personality disorders. They mistakenly believe that this will motivate them to behave better. Telling them this is not advised. Remember everything that has been said in the prior chapter: they don't have self-reflection and instead respond defensively; they are stuck trying to prove that they are right and that others have wronged them in the past; and they have great difficulty managing upset emotions.

Most mediators already know not to do this under ordinary circumstance. However, it is sometimes harder to remember when dealing with one or more high conflict clients. Just remember, this will save you a lot of future stress.

Conclusion

This chapter describes four things to forget about—to NOT DO—when working with high conflict mediation clients. Most of this is counter-intuitive and the opposite of what you feel like doing. Remembering the Four Fuhgeddaboudits is a good place to start.

CHAPTER 4

Preparing Yourself

It's not always obvious that you are going to be dealing with a high conflict mediation. Sometimes you will know what's coming because you have already interacted briefly with the parties individually, perhaps over the phone or in a pre-mediation coaching session. Or someone else may have told you to expect high conflict behavior. But in many cases, you will be surprised to discover this in the middle of the mediation process, because most high conflict people have learned to start out very friendly or charming and save their extreme behavior for later. We have learned to always be prepared for this possibility and have an idea of how you will deal with it.

One approach is to start all of your mediations as if they are going to be high conflict and use the simple structure of the *New Ways for Mediation* method described in Section II of this book. It is designed to help you maintain your balance and control throughout the process. If you realize that your clients are reasonable people, then you can always loosen up the process and use your full range of skills.

Another approach is to do your mediation in your usual way but have some high conflict techniques handy to use at any time, if necessary.

Spotting High Conflict People

How do you know whether you are entering into a mediation with one or more high conflict people? There is no way to know for sure, but you may find it helpful to use the *WEB Method*® we have developed. It's simple. Pay attention to:

Their **Words**: Do they speak in all-or-nothing terms? Lots of blaming words? Are they preoccupied with describing the other person's behavior with no mention of their own? Do they use words that take responsibility or not for being in the situation, if not for the problems within the situation? And, of course, do they write (and speak) IN ALL CAPITAL LETTERS? Can they speak for half an hour or more blaming the other party, without ever reflecting on their own behavior? (I shouldn't have hired him, married him, stayed in the job, etc.)

Your **Emotions**: Do you feel extreme emotions? Attacked? Insulted? Belittled? Dominated? In danger? Or do you feel extremely positive about one of the parties, as if they could become a best friend? (That's a warning sign, too, because of their charming first impressions!) Do you feel idealized by one of the parties, then suddenly devalued?

Their **Behavior**: Do they have a pattern of extreme behavior or making threats? Have they done something that 90% of people would never do? (That is usually an indication of an underlying pattern that supports extreme behavior.) Lying about important matters? Hiding or destroying property? Publicly humiliating the other party? Assaulting or alleged to have assaulted someone else? Have they brought lots of lawsuits against others? Or had lots of lawsuits brought against them?

None of this tells you for certain if you are dealing with a high conflict person. Sometimes you are just dealing with one or more parties who are upset about their issues and don't have a personality pattern of high conflict. But we have found that the *WEB Method* can help you make an educated guess earlier in the process. And since you can adapt your approach and use the techniques in this book with anyone, you might just use them if you are unsure.

One or Two HCPs?

One of the questions that often arises is whether you are dealing with one HCP or two—or even more in a case with several people involved. From our surveys of mediators, lawyers, judges, and others at our trainings, they report that about half of high conflict cases have two HCPs and half have only one, with the other person being fairly reasonable most of the time (although they may mirror the high conflict behavior in an effort to defend themselves). However, since you can use the methods described in this book with anyone, you never have to know whether it is one or both parties.

In fact, it is very important to maintain a neutral outlook regarding this question, otherwise you may be tempted to treat one or the other party as high conflict who isn't or treat one as reasonable who is actually high conflict. Sometimes this never becomes clear and sometimes it turns out to be the opposite of what you originally thought. So, the benefit of spotting the *possibility* of a high conflict person in your mediation is that you can adapt your approach to both parties as we describe in this book.

Three Theories of the High Conflict Case

Be cautious about believing or disbelieving one party's allegations that the other party is acting very badly. Some professionals jump to a conclusion that these allegations are usually true, while others jump to the conclusion that such statements are usually false. Many mediators tend to assume that both parties are equally acting badly. Any of these assumptions should be avoided and the mediator should keep a very open mind. This is not always easy in high conflict cases, but it is essential because your theory of the case influences how you treat the parties.

You should avoid *confirmatory bias,* which occurs when someone has only one theory of a case. The result is that you will tend to ignore information that doesn't fit, overvalue information that does fit, and misinterpret ambiguous information in favor of your theory. This confirmation bias will also lead you to try to convince the parties that your analysis is the correct one.

Keep in mind that HCPs can be *persuasive blamers,* meaning that their intense emotions can persuade you that they are the victim of the other party's terrible behavior when, in fact, it is the other way around. We have heard many complaints from people who have told us that they had a mediator who took one person's side throughout the case and never realized what was really happening.

One of the most common complaints is that the mediator never caught on to how one party was manipulating or blatantly lying throughout the mediation. Of course, these reports could also be inaccurate distortions of what the mediator really did or thought.

The safest approach is to always consider three theories of the high conflict case, as described below, and treat all parties in the same way throughout the process.

Three Theories of the High Conflict Case

A. Person B says Person A is acting badly and may be an HCP. It may be true.

B. Person B says Person A is acting badly, but Person B is actually acting badly, not Person A. Person B may be projecting their own thoughts, feelings, or behavior onto Person A. Person B may be an HCP and Person A is not.

C. Both Person A and Person B are acting badly. Both may be HCPs.

On the surface, the facts in all three scenarios are the same. You would have to look deeply beneath the surface to find out, but as mediators that is not our job. Instead, keep an open mind and a strong commitment to staying neutral throughout the case. Treat all parties the same.

Other High Conflict People

There is also the possibility that one or more family members and even professionals involved in the case is a high conflict person. Be careful to manage your dealings with them in a neutral manner as well. Avoid telling someone in the case that someone else is probably a high conflict person, because this news has a way of getting back to the person—whether they are a client, family member or professional.

What we have learned is that personality problems (high conflict and/or personality disorders) are unrelated to geography, intelligence or occupation. They are everywhere. When a professional exhibits the signs of being an HCP, use the same basic techniques that you would use with a mediation client, in terms of respect, caution and problem-solving.

Be prepared for this and don't be surprised. In many cases, you can find a way to work with the professionals involved that will help resolve the dispute.

Negative Advocates

Negative advocate is a term that Bill coined twenty years ago in his first book to describe the *enabling* behavior of such professionals, family members, and others who tried to protect or defend a high conflict person's negative behavior, thinking, and emotions. Such advocates have become a very common occurrence in high conflict disputes. Since HCPs lack good problem-solving skills, they tend to rely heavily on others to solve their problems for them demanding that they "do something" about the horrible person on the other side of the conflict (who is really their target of blame and may be totally innocent of their accusations).

Even reasonable people can become negative advocates when they feel swept up in an HCP's frequent emotional outbursts and demands. In many cases, such family members, professionals and others come to believe that the intense emotions of the HCP are *caused* by the other party—their target of blame. It's easy to feel persuaded of this as HCPs can be very *persuasive blamers*. Yet this usually comes from the internal workings of the HCP and has nothing to do with the real behavior of their target of blame.

It's important that you recognize this possibility so that you don't inadvertently become critical or even join in making judgments of their target of blame. The worst that sometimes happens in mediations is when the mediator becomes emotionally hooked by the HCP and their negative advocates and inappropriately puts pressure on their target of blame to accept responsibility for the dispute and agree to the HCP's demands. This pressure can be increased by their negative advocates (especially if they are their professionals) and should be carefully avoided.

It helps to be prepared for the presence of negative advocates in the dispute, so that you can decide how you want to deal with them. Sometimes it helps to keep them outside of the mediation process and sometimes it helps to include them so that you can educate them about the realities of the dispute and how they can help resolve it.

The key to understanding negative advocates is that they are emotionally hooked but uninformed. That is why they can be so intensely involved even when they are so wrong about understanding the situation. In many cases, negative advocates abandon the HCP once they eventually understand their role in feeding or creating the conflict. If you have the opportunity to involve them in discussions of the case (inside or outside of mediation sessions with the clients), they sometimes can become positive advocates and helpful to resolving the case once they realize the bigger picture of what is happening and the role of their HCP in it.

Positive Advocates

On the other hand, many high conflict people have positive advocates in their lives who actually help them manage their many conflicts in generally positive ways. These may be people who calm them down when HCPs are upset, or connect them to helpful resources, or give them good suggestions for resolving their case—without taking responsibility for it.

We have had many cases in which someone was a positive advocate—as friend or family member—who assisted in the case without becoming a negative advocate for the HCP. But it is often hard to tell in advance which you are dealing with. In general, HCPs have many negative advocates (more than positive advocates), so it is good to be prepared for them and have a strategy for excluding or managing them if they show up at your mediation.

Putting on Your Armor (Encouraging Statements)

We have found it useful to prepare for potentially high conflict mediations by reminding ourselves of certain short encouraging statements that we can remember under stress, which can be thought of as putting on your armor before going into a mediation. Here are several that we use and repeat to ourselves regularly:

It's not about you!

Their conflicts and criticisms—even of you—are about their personalities and lack of self-management skills. At times they may intensely blame you, as well as each other. Don't take this personally. (Yes, we know that's not easy at first!) It's not about you. Instead, stay focused on them, where you are in the structure of your mediation, and which skills to use at the time to manage them. As we will explain, HCPs have a lot of resistance to what will actually help them. We will show how you can address this while maintaining the momentum of your mediation.

In the middle of one mediation as the mediator tried to re-direct the parties to be more productive, they both turned

36

to the mediator and said "You're not helping!" Rather than get defensive, the mediator kept the focus on the parties and said "It sounds like you're frustrated with the way we're addressing this topic. Do you want to change topics now or do you want to take a different approach to this one? It's up to the two of you." They agreed to go on to the next topic for a while.

Moral to the story? High conflict people often get stuck in their arguments and can't stop themselves. When they are frustrated, they will often blame whoever is closest to them, including their professionals.

The issue's not the issue; the personality is the issue.
Often it seems really strange that your clients are fighting over an issue that seems quite simple or small. It's more complicated for them than the issue at hand. They often are feeling abandoned, disrespected, or dominated by the other party and this may drive their approach to individual issues or the whole dispute. This may be a feeling inside that does not fit the situation at all, but they perceive it that way.

Finalizing a settlement may represent no longer having contact with a person they still love or accepting the reality of a major financial loss. Therefore, they keep finding issues to fight about so they don't have to let go. In many cases, the dispute becomes the central issue in their daily lives and fighting over it gives them a sense of purpose in life.

You're not responsible for the outcome.
This is very important because it will help you stay focused on the process of the mediation, rather than feeling responsible to come up with solutions that the parties should really create. You're only responsible for your *standard of care* (a legal term meaning the standards, laws, and ethics that have been established for your profession in your community). No professional is responsible for the final outcome of a dispute.

Reminding yourself of this will help you avoid pushing any particular outcome onto the parties, which they will feel compelled to resist or, on the other hand, will adopt and then blame you for it. This will also help you when you see them moving backwards in the mediation, possibly undoing some previous agreements (which is common with

HCPs). Stay calm and keep exploring their issues in the same manner as when they address new issues.

Change how they think? Fuhgeddaboudit!

In the Chapter 3 we addressed the four fuhgeddaboudits. The key here is that you are not going to change how they think. By definition, personality disorders have enduring patterns of dysfunctional interpersonal behavior. You're not going to save them from growing up with a lifetime of self-defeating thoughts. But you may be able to help them resolve the dispute at hand even without changing their fundamental thinking or personalities.

It's a dilemma for the parties to resolve.

It's common for high conflict people to put the burden of resolving an issue on the mediator's shoulders. "What are you going to do about such-and-such problem, Ms. Mediator?" Rather than feeling the burden of figuring this out, put it right back on the parties' shoulders. "Well, actually you two have a dilemma. There are several ways you could resolve this. Let's look at your options, then you two can decide."

Tell them: "It's up to you!"

Because they often resist what will help them move forward, it's important to avoid getting into a power struggle with them about it. When they resist something, explain the benefits, then point out that it's up to them. You can say "This is how this is usually done, but it's up to you. Of course, if you don't do certain tasks, you won't be able to get your case resolved."

> In preparing for a divorce mediation session, a lawyer was preparing a financial disclosure form that needed to be exchanged between the parties. The client told her lawyer that she had $50,000 of separate property jewelry in another country which she did not plan on disclosing on the mandatory form. Her lawyer matter-of-factly pointed out that disclosing all property, separate and community, was a requirement of the disclosure process in order to get divorced, so that the other party could ask questions about it if they had any doubts about where the money came from to purchase that. Her lawyer said that he could not assist her in exchanging an incorrect form.

She insisted that she would not include the jewelry, so the lawyer said she would need to get a different lawyer or represent herself, but that he could not submit such a form. She had a choice. "It's up to you," he said. She decided to get a new lawyer.

Moral to the story? Keep these decisions on the client's shoulders, rather than getting into a heated argument or firing the client and getting blamed for abandoning her. While this example is about a lawyer and client before a mediation, the same principle applies with any high conflict client in mediation or other conflict resolution setting.

Conclusion

While it may feel difficult at times, it's essential to stay carefully neutral in mediating a dispute between one or more high conflict people. Preparing yourself for predictable problems will make your job easier because you won't be surprised and you can have solutions in mind from the start. There is great pressure from HCPs to get a mediator to take sides, so it must be clear from the start that this is not your job. Treating all parties and their advocates, if any, with respect and equal treatment will save you a lot of grief later in the case.

Most high conflict people accept that your role is to be balanced and neutral once you have made it clear from the start but they may occasionally need reminding from time to time. You can also remind yourself of key principles or short phrases as a way to manage yourself as you prepare for a successful mediation with potentially high conflict people.

SECTION 2

The
New Ways for Mediation
Method

The *New Ways for Mediation* method has a very simple structure. This is a necessity when dealing with potentially high conflict people. It makes it easier for them to focus on taking a problem-solving role and it makes it easier for the mediator to concentrate on guiding them. Section II explains how to implement this structure and how to manage many common challenges.

Stage of Mediation Process		Client Mediation Task
Stage 1: Establishing the Process	→	Asking Questions
Stage 2: Making the Agenda	→	Making Their Agenda
Stage 3: Making Proposals	→	Making Their Proposals
Stage 4: Making Decisions	→	Making Their Decisions

CHAPTER 5

Setting Up the Mediation

When setting up a potentially high conflict mediation there are several decisions you will need to make.

Pre-Mediation Coaching? Should there be pre-mediation coaching? (See Chapter 11 for more detail on this topic.) This is strongly recommended if you have been warned by a referral source, intake person, or one of the parties, that there will be a high conflict person present. Such coaching will help you determine whether it sounds like one or the other party or both are high conflict people. This may also help you decide whether to meet with them jointly or separately, and in person or by videoconferencing. But many mediators do not use pre-mediation coaching based on the nature of the dispute and will choose to proceed directly to the joint mediation session.

If there is pre-mediation coaching, who should do it? It's common for the mediator to do this, as it's easy to coordinate and the mediator gets better acquainted with each party beforehand, which can be very helpful in potentially high conflict cases. However, some people have pre-mediation coaching with their own lawyer or with a therapist. Some professionals specialize in offering pre-mediation coaching, so there are several options to consider.

Meeting jointly or by shuttle mediation? Many mediators choose to meet with their parties separately in shuttle mediation from the start if they expect a high conflict situation, such as in personal injury cases, heated business disputes, in elder or estate mediations, or in some difficult divorces. The key question is whether there is likely to be an ongoing relationship. If so, it is generally recommended to meet in person as much as possible, so that the parties strengthen their relationship with tools learned and practiced in the mediation. If emotions get too tense, then the mediator can caucus separately with each party for an appropriate amount of time to discuss a particularly troublesome issue, then get back together with both parties.

In high conflict relationship mediations (family, workplace, etc.), we have found that more caucuses are necessary than in ordinary mediation, but that it is still worthwhile attempting to work with them together most of the time. In extreme cases, it is better to simply do shuttle the entire time if the parties really can't stand each other and will not be working together in the future. (Bill has had cases in which the parties' lawyers couldn't stand to be in the same room, so that the whole mediation was done by shuttle in separate rooms.)

Meeting in-person or videoconferencing? During the coronavirus, videoconferencing was widely available while in-person mediation was not an option. Yet as communities return to the option of in-person mediation, many people may still prefer videoconferencing. Here are some considerations:

In-person mediation offers the ability to feel more connected by sharing the same physical space. For mediators, this gives the option of more accurately reading body language and knowing what (or who else) is in the client's immediate environment. In some ways, the mediator can be more nurturing in-person, by offering snacks, tissues, and their own full-body language of openness and interest in the clients. It also takes longer for an upset person to storm out of a room (with the chance of getting them to reconsider), than for them to simply drop out of a video meeting. Also, lighting and sound (and Wi-Fi signals) are much easier to manage in-person than in a video meeting.

On the other hand, videoconferencing offers a sense of more distance from the other party and the comfort of appearing from one's own home (or office). Likewise, there is the convenience of not having to drive across a big city and also the option of working with a mediator who lives hundreds of miles away. While lawyers and therapists are generally licensed to only work with clients in their own states, most mediators are not subject to regional rules and regulations at this time. But a mediator should find out their legal status if they want to work outside of their own state by videoconferencing, just to be certain.

Violence concerns? For mediators handling divorce cases, they are strongly encouraged to do separate pre-mediation screening sessions with each party to assess for domestic violence (also known as *intimate partner violence*). (See Chapter 11) In some areas, such screening may be a legal requirement or the community's *standard of care* expectation.

This concern can also exist in workplace mediation, business mediation, and any other mediation. Here is a very disturbing example in a business dispute:

> A subcontractor was suing a company for no longer wanting the subcontractor's services. A business mediation was scheduled at a mediator's law office. A while before the mediation, the lawyer for the CEO of the company received the following message from the disgruntled subcontractor:
>
> "I am going after you with every fiber in my being and I won't rest until I see you behind bars for conspiracy to defraud."
>
> Apparently, the subcontractor repeatedly swore at and threatened the lawyer for weeks before the mediation. He also had a history of being a bully and suing many other people.
>
> On the day of the mediation, the CEO, the CEO's lawyer, and the subcontractor (representing himself) met with the mediator but did not reach an agreement. On the way out of the building, the subcontractor pulled out a gun and shot and killed the lawyer and the CEO. The next day the man killed himself. The mediator was unharmed.[10]

While very rare, this is a cautionary example of taking risk of violence seriously in today's world, including in potentially high conflict mediation. In the case above, we see language that would fulfill some of the warning signs of the WEB Method described in Chapter 3: *preoccupation with blaming, all-or-nothing thinking, unmanaged emotions,* and *extreme behavior or threats.*

What should have been done in this case? The mediation should have been canceled or held in a secure location, such as at a courthouse or law office with metal detectors. Of course, the mediator did not know that the lawyer was getting messages like this. But if there had been some form of pre-mediation separate session, the lawyer might have mentioned these threats and the mediator might have taken precautions.

Domestic Violence Precautions? In divorce or child custody cases where there has been domestic violence, mediation may still be appropriate in some cases if sufficient precautions are taken. These can include: shuttle in videoconferencing by using virtual breakout rooms; in-person shuttle mediation with the mediator going between rooms; having parties arrive and leave separately (with the alleged abuser arriving first and leaving last); having a cue for a victim/survivor to give the mediator if they stop feeling safe; having a metal detector. (See screening in Chapter 11: Pre-Mediation Coaching.)

Co-Mediation? Some mediators like to do co-mediation and some community mediation programs regularly have co-mediators. Sometimes a lawyer and a therapist will do co-mediation in divorce or family business disputes. This can work well when the co-mediators are working well together. It helps to plan ahead before the mediation for possible high conflict behavior and agree on who will take responsibility for which tasks.

For example, one co-mediator might lead the discussion while the other is taking notes and watching for uncomfortable body language. Or one co-mediator might take the lead on one topic and the other might take the lead on another topic. If there are possible negative advocates (see Chapter 3) for an HCP present, one co-mediator may need to meet with them separately at some point or just keep an eye on them to see if they are becoming upset. The main issue is that co-mediators are in agreement and comfortable with each other's role.

Splitting? Sometimes, an HCP will attempt to form an alliance with one of the co-mediators to get him or her to take the HCP's side. High conflict people routinely (and unconsciously) will try to *split* the professionals, viewing one as really good and the other as really bad. They are hoping to get one professional to become an advocate for them. Unfortunately, an unwary mediator can fall for this and become a negative advocate, trying to convince the other co-mediator to go easy on that client. This can create tension between the co-mediators and they often don't know what happened. Splitting can be very subtle and divisive. Prepare for this by agreeing to watch out for it before the mediation begins and agree not to argue about it in front of the parties. Just take a break if there is a concern.

Conclusion

Setting up the mediation includes addressing many questions, especially when there is the possibility of a high conflict person included in the mediation. Each of these questions may have different answers for different mediations. The main thing is that you address them one way or another with realistic thinking about each specific mediation.

Pre-mediation coaching is encouraged when high conflict people might be involved. Taking appropriate precautions against risks of violence must always be considered when emotions are running high. When in doubt, be more structured rather than less.

CHAPTER 6

New Skills and Tasks

The *New Ways for Mediation* method emphasizes new skills and tasks (new *ways*) for the clients in dispute resolution. The new *skills* are:

- *managed emotions*
- *flexible thinking*
- *moderate behavior,* and
- *checking themselves*

Ideally, these self-management skills are taught prior to the mediation. These are described in more depth in Chapter 11: Pre-Mediation Coaching and Chapter 12: Pre-Mediation Programs.

The four client mediation *tasks* are used throughout the mediation process and can be taught before or during the mediation:

Stage of Mediation Process		Client Mediation Task
Stage 1: Establishing the Process	→	Asking Questions
Stage 2: Making the Agenda	→	Making Their Agenda
Stage 3: Making Proposals	→	Making Their Proposals
Stage 4: Making Decisions	→	Making Their Decisions

These tasks are easy to teach and apply during the mediation. You just have to be persistent in guiding the clients to do them. By keeping the parties focused on doing these tasks to resolve their own dispute, they are less emotionally reactive, less preoccupied with blaming, less focused on the past, and get the credit for finding and following their own solutions.

This means that the mediator must be very directive about the process of the mediation, while remaining very non-directive about the outcome. It helps to develop the mindset that you are not focused on *whether* they reach an agreement, but on *how* they reach their agreement. This way they feel the responsibility of working hard to move past their dispute rather than simply resisting each other and the mediator.

There is a key principle here: *Don't work harder than your clients.* If you do, then your clients will not work hard at problem-solving, but rather will be busy defending themselves and attacking each other while waiting on you to solve things for them. Using the four client mediation tasks described here, the mediator can reinforce their *logical thinking* rather than their *emotional reacting*.

Four Client Mediation Tasks

All of these tasks are designed to shift them from high conflict thinking and behavior into problem-solving. They are designed to be simple to use with the mediator's strong guidance. How to implement teaching and reinforcing these tasks in the mediation will be explained stage-by-stage in the next four chapters. Here is an introduction to the tasks and the reasoning for each:

Asking Questions

This may seem unimportant or unnecessary; however, it is essential in helping the parties focus away from emotional reactions onto problem-solving. In many high conflict disputes, one or more parties may come in very demanding from the start and insisting on what he or she thinks the mediator should do. By emphasizing the clients' role in asking questions, it helps shift the role of the mediator from being seen as a potential tool or negative advocate for either high conflict party to being seen as a source of information and expertise.

By explaining this task right away near the start of the mediation, the mediator can convey to the parties the idea that this is a joint project in problem-solving which will involve the best thinking of everyone. Thinking of questions to ask will keep them busy moving toward finding solutions.

This also helps the mediator know where the parties are coming from, what knowledge they have about the process, and what is important to them. It helps to regularly ask them if they have any questions about this or that. At first, they often do not have questions, but sooner or later they usually start asking and it helps focus the parties on information they can gather for finding their solutions. It helps in developing a sense of teamwork among the parties and the mediator.

Making Their Agenda

This is a huge paradigm shift for many mediators. Each of us was trained in having the mediator make the agenda and did that for many years. However, this is another key area in which to keep the parties thinking about problem-solving, rather than just emotionally reacting. By having them bring a list of proposed agenda items, they will be more efficient and constructive during the mediation.

Another benefit of this is that high conflict clients tend to go off their agenda as they emotionally react to each other's statements and proposals and bring in more and more related or unrelated issues in an effort to *win* the issue at hand. So, instead of the mediator struggling with them to get them back to the mediator's agenda, the mediator can help them stick with *their own agenda*.

For example, if the parties have raised new issues, the mediator can say: *"Now you were talking about the child support issue, but you just started bringing up a drinking issue. Both of these can be important. So, do you want to stick with your agenda item and save this for later, or switch to this new topic now? It's up to the two of you."*

This approach helps the mediator remain strictly neutral, even about which agenda item to discuss. It requires the parties to think about the process and not just about their arguments. This also helps the mediator stay in control of the process, because you have the support of the parties in directing the discussion back to their chosen topic rather than opposition to your chosen topic.

Making Their Proposals

This task is the centerpiece of high conflict mediation and can be productively used in any mediation or negotiation with anyone anywhere. By thinking of proposals, the parties really do have to *think* instead of *reacting*. They can think of these before they come into the mediation, and certainly during the mediation.

This task contains three steps:

1. **One person (the proposer) makes a proposal.** Either person can make a proposal. This can simply include Who will do What, When and Where. This could be one tiny item or a full package proposal of a deal involving many terms. Sometimes people bring written proposals to consider, depending on the nature of the dispute and the readiness of the parties. Sometimes it is better to have one small item to address in a high conflict case, and other times it's better to have a full package so that the other can see that it includes benefits as well as disappointments.

2. **The other person (the respondent) asks questions about it.** This is the hardest part of the whole mediation. In high conflict cases, one or both parties will be very reactive. When they hear a proposal, their immediate reaction is usually anger: "How could you make such a proposal!" "Why did you think I would ever agree to that?" "Now you say it! Why didn't you bring that up a year ago, when we could have saved thousands of dollars!" And on and on.

    This small skill needs to be tightly guided by the mediator. When presenting the proposal process, the mediator needs to say: "It will be very important to ask questions containing Who, What, Where, and When. Try to avoid Why questions because they are really criticisms in disguise. For example, 'Why did you think I would ever agree to that!' Or: 'Why didn't you suggest that a year ago!'"

    In role play exercises, we have had people say that they could feel their brain shifting gears while practicing this skill, from criticizing the other person to thinking of a good question. It really seems to shift the person out of emotional reactions and into logical thinking. We have witnessed this happen in many cases.

    Then, the person who made the proposal answers these questions. This is when these skills can really make the difference. If the mediator is successful at reinforcing the use of questions and answers at this step, everything else usually follows more logically and productively. If the mediator does not reinforce the use of respectful questions and answers at this step, the process can quickly spin out of control. This will be discussed in more depth in Chapter 9: Stage 3 – Making Proposals.

3. **Then, the other person (respondent) says "Yes," "No," or "I'll Think About It."** After the respondent's questions have been answered, all the respondent needs to say is "Yes, I can do that." Or: "No, I don't agree." Or: "I'll think about it." That is all they need to say. With Yes, you can focus on writing down the terms and filling in any added details. With No, then the other person (respondent) now becomes the proposer and makes a new proposal.

It is important to know that "I'll think about it" is a really good answer in a high conflict case, because it means they are thinking and not emotionally reacting and rejecting the proposal out of hand. The mediator just has to keep track of how long they need to think about it.

By having the respondent who says "No" become the next proposer, you avoid having the respondent just sit there and reject proposals one after another without also having to do the thinking.

This task and these steps are the focus of Chapter 9. Successfully managing this proposal process is often the turning point in a high conflict case.

Making Their Decisions

This task is often assumed in mediations but needs to be thought of as an important skill to develop and reinforce for the parties. If one or both are high conflict people, then they are used to conflict without resolution—just constant disagreements and frustration—without actually making final decisions. Also, high conflict people are used to regretting their decisions soon after they have made them.

In some cases, one party initiates legal action to try to set aside one of their decisions (usually unsuccessfully) and in other cases they simply do not carry out their agreement. In many cases, it is just one person who undermines the agreement, but there are also cases in which both parties refuse to follow it (often blaming the other person's non-compliance). Sometimes they end up back in court for this reason. We want to avoid this.

Therefore, it is important to raise all the possible details that would be involved in implementing the decision that the parties can think of and that the mediator can think of (after the parties have done their thinking first). Another concern is thinking of what should be done if the agreement is not carried out.

Then, it often helps to get the parties thinking of how likely they are to actually follow through with their decisions. If they realize that one or the other party is unlikely to follow through, then they should think of what could be done to make it a stronger agreement now, rather than waiting to see it fall apart later. Remember that high conflict people are not used to ending their conflicts.

As you can see, each of these tasks has smaller tasks within it that can help create more solid decisions. But you do not need to explain that to the parties. Just keep it simple for them as the four client tasks for a successful mediation.

Skills for Mediators

The key skills for mediators to use in high conflict mediation are not necessarily new, but there is a shift in emphasis as compared to the skills mediators use in normal mediations. This is where it is important to remember the Four Fuhgeddaboudits from Chapter 3:

FUHGEDDABOUD:
1. trying to give the parties insights into their own behavior
2. focusing on the past
3. emotional confrontations or discussions of emotions
4. telling them they have a high conflict personality

Instead, the three key skills for mediators are actually very simple and easy to remember. However, they are hard to do for mediators who are used to trying to give the parties insights, focusing a lot on the past, and encouraging emotional exchanges. But that is okay. If the parties blow up at those methods, it is easy to see that the following three skills are the ones to emphasize:

1. Connect with Empathy, Attention and Respect
2. Structure the process
3. Educate the parties

The repetition of these three skills makes it easier to manage and guide a high conflict mediation than if you try to solve their problems for them. It really is a guiding process, with the mediator using all of his or her skills to remain connected, to stick with the structure and to educate them about all you have learned as a mediator from other cases and other background information you may have. This is the way to reinforce the parties using their four client mediation skills.

Connect with E.A.R.

Empathy, attention and respect are what most high conflict people want. In fact, they are often desperate to get these because most other people in their lives have stopped empathizing with them, stopped giving them attention, and stopped showing them respect. They often get the opposite of these from the people around them because of their own actions, but they cannot connect the dots back to their own high conflict behavior.

This skill for mediators is fairly simple. Think of it as an *EAR Statement*. It is something you can say and/or show with your body language. You can say these in a separate caucus or with the parties both together; just make sure you give them both an EAR Statement. They can include statements like any of the following:

EMPATHY: "I can hear your frustration about this."
"I can see this is a very stressful situation."
"I know these procedures can seem very confusing."
"I want to help you succeed here."

ATTENTION: "Tell me more. I want to understand."
"I'll take as much time as necessary to hear your concerns."
"You both deserve to be heard."
"I'll work with you on this."

RESPECT: "I really respect your efforts to resolve this."
"You are a good record-keeper. Thanks for this information."
"You have accomplished a lot already."
"You have both made some helpful proposals."

There are endless examples of statements that can show empathy, attention and/or respect. Any one of these types of EAR Statements can calm the conflict, or you can put two or three together, such as:

> *"I know this can be difficult. These are very important decisions in your life. (Empathy) Don't worry, I'll spend as much time with you as needed to understand and help you come up with proposals. (Attention) I have a lot of respect for the preparation that you have both made for this mediation session. (Respect)"*

If you are saying this to both parties, make sure to have good eye contact with each of them, even though it may mean looking back and forth occasionally. If you have given an EAR Statement to one party to calm them down, make sure to say an EAR Statement to the other party as well. But it does not have to be the same or take as long. You will know by their body language if you need to say more.

If you are doing shuttle mediation, it is easy to give EAR Statements tailored to that individual's needs. If you are doing a joint mediation, sometimes you may need to go into separate caucuses to hear them out more and to give them more EAR Statements.

Non-verbal behavior is very important here. Make sure you have a lot of eye contact with each party, nod your head with understanding when appropriate, lean in as you are listening, and have your arms and hands looking open, not defensive. You can even do this in virtual sessions!

It may help to clarify that giving such statements does not mean that you are agreeing or disagreeing with either one of them. You are trying to connect with both of them.

You will need to give EAR Statements several times during a mediation session. That is fine. It will help you stay connected to both parties.

From our experience, EAR Statements work at calming people within 30 seconds about 90% of the time. Sometimes it takes longer with higher doses of empathy, attention and/or respect. Sometimes, you will need to go into a caucus to really listen to each client and give them more EAR Statements. In some cases, it may be best to simply move on to the next task even though one or both parties are still somewhat upset.

Occasionally, someone may challenge you on your empathy, attention, or respect ("Don't patronize me!"). To that, we usually respond: "I'm just trying to help you. Let us move on now to the next task." It is hard for them to argue that you're not trying to help them.

Structure the Process

This is a skill that is more necessary with high conflict disputes. The process needs to be more tightly structured, so that the parties do not slip back into their attack and defend cycles. However, this also does not have to be hard. You just need to be clear, consistent and firm about it.

Part of this is enforcing the stage of the mediation that you are in. It also means getting comfortable with more quickly interrupting the client's negative or diversionary comments and re-directing them back to the task at hand. EAR Statements help a lot here. Many mediators tell us they feel rude interrupting the clients so firmly with this method. But once they get used to it, they say that it really is not very hard, and they find it very effective.

The reason for this tighter structure (described in depth in the next four chapters) is that high conflict people cannot stop themselves. They lack the internal restraints and impulse control that most people have, and that they may have when they are not dealing with such personal issues. Yet when the outer environment structures them, they can be very successful at making proposals and reaching agreements.

However, keep in mind that when they are away from the structure of the mediation process, they often get in touch with their upset emotions again and want to undo the agreements they made when they were more structured and focused during the mediation. That is why it is important at the end of the process to address any predictable problems and get them settled (often in writing) as well.

Structuring the process requires several small skills:

Guiding proposals: At the center of the structure are their proposals. This was described above as a skill for them to use and will be described more in Chapter 9. However, thinking about their proposals will help the mediator structure the process in terms of:

- giving them information for making proposals (Stage 1)
- helping them make an agenda of issues (Stage 2)
- making their proposals and asking questions about them (Stage 3), and
- finalizing their agreements, usually in writing (Stage 4)

In many ways, the *New Ways for Mediation* structure helps the mediator think under the pressure of guiding high conflict clients as much as it helps the parties stay focused on problem-solving.

Re-direct them to What To Do: One of the key principles of psychology mixed into this process is that it is easier to get people to do something else than it is to get them to just stop what they are used to doing. This is the fundamental success of Alcoholics Anonymous: Instead of trying not to drink, go to a meeting and talk about it; see your friends; work the 12 steps; and so forth. Telling high conflict people to just stop interrupting or stop being angry or stop blaming each other does not work. What does work is to focus them on the task at hand or re-direct them to the next task, be it asking a question, gathering more information, making a proposal or whatever.

For example: Rather than telling them to stop blaming or stop talking about the past, just simply say: "So, what's your proposal about that?" No need to discipline them or argue about whether they were doing something wrong. No need to trigger their defensiveness. It is easier to do new than to stop doing old.

Addressing dilemmas: High conflict parties often feel helpless, stuck, and trapped. They will want to off-load responsibility for making decisions. At these times they are used to turning on each other in anger and may eventually turn on the mediator in anger as well. "What are you going to do about this problem!" they may say. Or they just give up in frustration and say "You decide! You tell us what to do!"

Don't ever decide or tell them what to do! You must keep the burden on them to resolve their dispute. Otherwise, they will blame you for doing it wrong, or say that you *made them* do something that they didn't want to do. Most lawsuits against mediators include language like this. Becoming directive about the outcome is to be avoided and there are many ways to do that which will be explained in the next few chapters.

Instead, at these times, you can turn to both of them and say: "You folks have a dilemma. How do you want to resolve this? Here are some possible solutions that others have used that might help you think about proposals for this situation." That way you resist the urge to simply make a decision for them and you keep responsibility for their decisions on their shoulders. This is an important part of *guiding the process* of high conflict mediation. Throughout the process they will try to off-load decision-making to you. Stay firm about this and gently keep it on their shoulders.

Managing disputes about the facts: Most reasonable people agree on the facts of a case and focus on what should be done. High conflict people tend to focus on the past and want to fight over the facts. This is where they have spent a lot of their lives: fighting over who did what to whom in the past. Memorize this phrase: "I cannot mediate the past." Remind them of that from the beginning of the mediation through to the end.

Trying to resolve the parties' disputes about the past is where many mediators lose control, and their clients give up and walk out. We have learned this from experience. Point out that they do not need to resolve the past; they need to make proposals about the future. They know the past and you do not need to know their past (which they don't agree on anyway). So, they just need to use their own knowledge and perspective on the past in making their proposals for the future. This is where the real action is. They can do it! You just have to encourage and re-direct them back to the present and making decisions about the future.

In re-directing them, you can simply say to each of them "*You* might be right, and *you* might be right. I'll never know. I wasn't there. But I do know that you can move forward in making your decisions about the present and the future regardless of the past." "You might be right" can save a lot of wasted time arguing about the past.

Emphasize their strengths: One of the common problems when dealing with high conflict people is that you may see all of their behavior as negative. They often see each other that way. It helps to regularly acknowledge positive efforts and gestures they may make, no matter how small. Make sure to make such comments to both parties, even if only one appears to be high conflict. Remember the three theories of the case: it could be one or the other or both. Emphasizing their strengths helps them stay calm and focused.

Giving them hope: Throughout the mediation process and throughout their lives, high conflict people feel hopeless. They tend to lack skills for successful problem-solving in close relationships. (They may be brilliant at other things, including their jobs.) And when they feel stuck, the mediator can often pick up that feeling as well. Do your best to give them hope.

From the start, they may express frustration about not telling their story about the past. YOU can say: "Many people have found this method really works for them, so hang in there and see how it goes." Regularly give them hope about their progress. "You've really made more progress than I expected for today." And: "I think you're closer to an agreement on this issue than you realize."

Try to avoid saying how bad things appear to be. Try to help them see the potential that they have. Many high conflict parties have resolved their disputes using methods such as this. And many parties have reached agreements after taking a break that they thought were impossible before the break. (Of course, the break may be ten minutes, ten days or ten months.)

Don't give up on them. It's better to admit that you're out of ideas, but you're willing to keep working with them if you can. When the clients are paying a private mediator, you usually have the ability to keep going. If they are involved in a limited program, then you can still wish them the best and let them know they can still make efforts to work it out themselves with the tools they have learned in the mediation (such as making proposals and asking questions about them).

Educating the Parties

The third main skill for mediators to use in mediating high conflict disputes is educating the parties. This too has several smaller skills within it, all of them quite easy and familiar. The biggest difference in this method from normal mediations is that the mediator doesn't ask probing, insight-oriented questions about the past, such as "What did you used to do? How did that work for you two?" This often leads to squabbling over whether it worked or not, and the parties are back into attack and defend territory. Avoid these questions as much as possible.

Instead, by focusing on educating the parties, the mediator can keep the discussion focused on options for what to do now. This also offers an opportunity for the mediator to share a lot of his or her information and knowledge in the subject area, if appropriate. In this regard, here are some smaller skills to use:

Educate them about standards and limitations: Depending on the nature of the dispute and the mediator's role, this can include legal information, financial information, parenting information, construction information, tax information, and so forth. But it all needs to be *information* and *not advice*. This information should be presented with extreme neutrality, so that the mediator is not perceived to be tilting it toward one party or the other.

This is very important for non-lawyer mediators. A review of many states' laws about "unauthorized practice of law" (UPL) focuses on whether the non-lawyer mediator *directed* the parties toward any particular law-based agreement. By emphasizing that this is just information and that they should seek legal counsel, a non-lawyer may be protected from such a concern. But notice the "may be" protected. It is best to learn the rules about UPL in your jurisdiction before risking violating them. And mediators who are also lawyers need to keep the same idea in mind: share information not advice. Keep the roles clear.

To the extent that you are allowed to talk about standards, it helps to educate the parties about general standards early in the process, before they make their proposals. This can help the mediator appear neutral rather than saying the law disallows or experience frowns on one of the parties' proposals *after* they have made it.

Refer to lawyers and experts: This follows from the prior discussion. Mediators who actively recommend that their clients speak to lawyers, accountants, evaluators, counselors and others, are doing a service to their clients—as well as protecting themselves. If you are making direct referrals, it is ideal to refer to at least three experts in the area. There have been some successful lawsuits (none regarding mediators to our knowledge) against professionals who made direct referrals to experts who then committed malpractice. If such a person was one of three you referred to, the client had an opportunity to interview and choose the one they did so there is less likelihood that this can be blamed on you. Check this out with a legal adviser in your area. Keep in mind that high conflict people are the ones most likely to sue their own professionals, although this is much less common with mediators.

Educate about options: This can be one of the most important parts of your mediation. By presenting options, you are giving them information that they may not have or have not considered. High conflict people often focus on one solution to the problem and defend it, rather than looking into several other options.

When you present options, try to have at least three for them to consider. That way you are not directing them to one solution, which one may like and the other does not like, so that they just get into an argument about it. Also, this avoids the appearance of you looking like you are telling them what to do. If you offer two options, then one client may like one and the other client may like the other. Again, you risk an unnecessary conflict. By offering three options, they really have to think about them without jumping to attack or defend one or two.

Deal with resistance: Throughout the mediation process with high conflict people, you will need to deal with their resistance to doing what ordinary people will easily do. "I don't want to fill out these forms." "I don't like your methods." "Are you sure you know what you're doing?" "You're not helping us at all!"

> In one case, a divorce mediation client brought in a book to the second mediation session and told the mediator "Here is the right way you are supposed to be doing mediation!" The mediator said he had actually seen that book years before. The book described a method of mediation designed to get the parties to reconcile. But the other party was extremely clear that he did not want to reconcile.
>
> The mediator said to the wife "I can understand that reconciliation is what you are looking for and it's sad that this is not what is happening now and that the marriage counseling did not work out. I am providing divorce mediation services which can help ease this transition for your whole family's benefit and your husband has made it clear this is what's happening now."

After the wife ran out of the mediation room and returned a couple times, the husband gave up on mediation and decided to go to court.

Moral of the story? You can't always succeed, even if you are very gentle and careful with the process. However, this also demonstrates how you can deal with resistance with a 2-Step, as explained below.

The 2-Step for Dealing with Resistance

Here is an easy way to deal with resistance, which is very common in high conflict cases:

STEP 1: Give a brief statement showing empathy, attention and respect for their concern.

STEP 2: Then, give a brief statement educating them on the issue.

The example above demonstrates these two steps with empathy (I can understand…it's sad) and education (I'm providing divorce mediation . . . it can ease this transition)

Another example: "I can understand that you don't want to fill out those financial forms. You may not be aware that our state requires those to be exchanged before a divorce can be completed."

Or: "I can see your frustration with this employment procedure. You may not be aware that unless you do this, your job could be in jeopardy because of the following policy…"

(Mediators in Texas want us to call this the "Texas 2-Step." We will leave that up to you.)

Educate about consequences: In many situations, high conflict people are oblivious to the consequences of their decisions when they are upset. For example, they may dramatically say: "Then let's just go to court!" Rather than feeling defeated or frustrated, you can simply say (2-step):

"I hear your frustrations with this. That is always one of your options. But you may want to consider what the cost and time delay will be with that. Have you spoken to a lawyer about the cost and time involved?"

Such a matter-of-fact educational approach often helps the client think twice and decide to keep going in mediation.

In general, with high conflict people (and many others), it helps to point out both positive and negative consequences of various options they are considering. The negative consequences are often easy to discuss, although the client(s) may never have known about them or thought about them. But the positive consequences may also be helpful because high conflict people often feel like all the consequences are negative and it may give them some hope and direction. If you just talk about negative consequences, it may be demoralizing. If you just talk about positive consequences, a high conflict person may not find you to be very realistic. That is why both positive and negative are important.

When it is time to write up their agreement or otherwise finalize its terms, it helps to talk about what should be done if they do not fulfill some of their decisions. This is another area for a consequences discussion. Should there be a financial penalty if certain terms are not fulfilled? Should the agreement be re-negotiated? Let the parties know about all the possible consequences they might consider, so that once the agreement is finalized, they are more motivated to fulfill it to avoid all the negative consequences and to get all the benefits.

Conclusion

The first part of this chapter focused on the four mediation skills for clients of:

1. Asking questions
2. Making their agenda
3 Making their proposals; and
4. Making their decisions

These are designed to maximize the parties' active involvement in thinking activities, rather that emotionally reacting to what the other party and the mediator say. They are relatively easy skills to teach but take a lot of guidance from the mediator to reinforce when the going gets tough during the mediation. Once the parties get used to these skills, some of them can start doing them on their own, while others will continue to need your guidance.

The second part of this chapter focused on three skills to emphasize for mediators. This means that mediators avoid the four fuhgeddaboudits and instead stay focused on these three forward-moving skills:

1. Connecting with EAR Statements
2. Structuring the process; and
3. Educating the parties

By practicing these three skills over and over again in the mediation, the mediator can guide the parties to steer clear of their past reactions to truly make their own decisions and get the credit for making them. This approach also seems to increase the likelihood that they will actually follow their agreements, which is a common problem with high conflict people.

We might add that you can use any or all of these skills with any clients in any mediation, not just high conflict ones. However, the normal skills that do work in normal mediations often do not work with high conflict people because they tend to emphasize insight, exploring the past, and opening up emotional issues.

The next four chapters address the four basic stages of the *New Ways for Mediation* method.

Stage 1: Establishing the Process

The *New Ways for Mediation* process is simple but needs to be firm from the start. The first stage sets the tone and focuses the parties' expectations on using their skills and engaging in their four tasks throughout the process. There are several key points to make as you introduce the mediation process, similar to those of a normal mediation. Certain common mediation practices will need more emphasis while others will be minimized or not used at all.

Establishing the process means much more than just explaining it. This includes establishing sufficient control from the start so that the parties don't hijack the process and use it to blame each other and block decision-making. Since high conflict people frequently lose emotional self-control, this means that you will need to keep coming back to this foundation of the mediator talking and the parties just listening.

Establishing the process also means teaching the clients to ask the mediator questions throughout the mediation, in order to shift the focus to problem-solving and away from venting and power struggles when they flare up. This also means establishing your gentle authority to keep the parties in each Stage of the mediation, so they don't jump from topic to topic unnecessarily.

Here are the general principles that need to be emphasized:

Explain the Process

At the start of the mediation, after appropriate brief chit chat, it is important for the mediator to talk and the parties to listen. This is especially true with high conflict clients, who often try to start the session by making demands or complaints about the other party or the mediation process. Here are some common ones we've heard:

"My girlfriend is outside. Can she come in the mediation?"

"How long will this take? I only put one hour in the parking meter."

"I refuse to pay for this. It's all his fault."

"Do you know what he just said before we came in? Let me tell you!"

Do not get distracted by attempts to hijack your process. Calmly insist on addressing any diversionary issues *after* you have explained your mediation process.

"We will get to those types of concerns shortly. First, I have to explain the process to you, so you'll know what to expect and what your part is. This will be very brief. It's what I've found to be the most helpful to do. So, I appreciate your patience. Thanks."

This can be hard at first, especially for new mediators. It is tempting to be nice and friendly and start listening to and discussing these early demands and complaints. But be reassuring and use your EAR Statements while you re-direct the conversation to what you need to tell them to get started.

Having the mediator talk first establishes two important things:

1. The mediator establishes control over who talks and who listens, which is a necessary foundation for maintaining control or re-gaining control during the mediation's rough spots with potentially high conflict clients.

2. It gets the parties *thinking.* Thinking about the process rather than their upset emotions.

Of course, many (perhaps the majority of) high conflict clients do not show their upset emotions and lack of self-restraint at the start and may be quite cooperative at first, waiting to see how things are going to go.

The following is the introduction that Bill has used for the past ten years for his divorce mediations, which usually do not have lawyers present and two-thirds do not have lawyers at all. This can easily be adapted to any type of mediation:

> "*Welcome to mediation. Before we get started, I want to point out three key things about my mediation process:*
>
> *Number 1 and most important: You folks are the decision-makers. So I won't make your decisions for you, I won't pressure you to make any particular decisions, and I won't pressure you in terms of time, except that we have ___ hours set aside for your mediation today. And I won't pressure you to even make an agreement. That is always up to each of you. I'm in charge of the process and you're in charge of making your decisions.*
>
> *Number 2: I am a lawyer [could be any other type of professional—or not], but I won't be giving you any legal advice now or ever. You are and always will be mediation clients for me. It's one hat per case and this case uses my mediator hat. However, you should feel free to ask me any general questions about standards and I will answer with information, not advice, whenever I can. I always encourage you to get legal advice or other consultation on the issues involved.*
>
> *Do either of you have a lawyer who represents you and will need to sign the final agreement? I don't need to know if you have just consulted with a lawyer.*
>
> *Number 3: You should know that judges and the courts encourage you to make agreements in mediation rather than to have them decide. They know that you know your case better than anyone and will have more time in mediation to discuss and resolve issues than you would have in court.*
>
> *Any questions about those three things?" [They usually don't but occasionally they do.]*

Then there is a discussion of the standard mediation ground rules of confidentiality, impartiality, and other issues about the mechanics of the mediation process, including emphasizing the following points.

Explain the Mediator's Role

This is essentially the same as in a normal mediation, but in high conflict mediation you need to really emphasize that you will be neutral, will not give them advice and will not decide if proposals and agreements are *fair* or *reasonable*. It can help to spell out these concerns and answer them, even if the clients didn't ask:

> *"Some of my clients think I am like a judge, who will decide who is right and who is wrong. But that is not what we do in mediation. I really am neutral and not the decision-maker."*

> *"Some clients think I should give them advice about the law because I am a lawyer. I am not in that role in this mediation process. Talk to separate lawyers and other experts if you want advice. At most, I can give you general information related to your dispute, if I even know it."*

> *"Some clients really expect me to pass judgment on their proposals regarding how fair they are. In mediation, the parties need to decide that and get outside advice or opinions on fairness and reasonableness. If you are unable to decide what is fair, you should have an advocate of some sort in the mediation or simply work through lawyers or other people. I am not allowed to be the judge of what's fair or reasonable as a mediator."*

By raising these types of thoughts (which they often have without saying so), you can head off common misunderstandings that high conflict people have because of their frequent cognitive distortions. It may be helpful to have something in writing that explains this to the clients before (such as in a scheduling letter) or during the mediation.

On the other hand, explain what you will be doing. You will:

- be a guide for the whole mediation process
- answer their questions
- be a source of information about what others have done, and
- facilitate them in making their proposals and otherwise using their skills to reach agreements

> *"My job includes maintaining control of the process, like a traffic cop who decides whose turn it is to drive through the intersection. I may interrupt from time to time to help you stay on course. But I would encourage you to avoid interrupting each other as much as possible."*

Explain the Clients' Role

This is when you introduce the 4 Client Mediation Skills, as explained in the prior chapter:

1. Asking questions
2. Making their agenda
3. Making their proposals
4. Making their agreements

Asking questions: This does not need to be very in-depth at the beginning, as you will explain each of these in more detail when it's time to use them. But explain asking questions right away, because this will be important in helping them help themselves from the start of the process.

> *"Since this is a process that depends a lot on your proposals, I encourage you to ask me questions at any time during the process. A lot of this mediation may be confusing or different from another mediation you may have had. Do you have any questions about this so far? Have either of you been in mediation before?"*

As explained in the prior chapter, asking questions is an important step for high conflict people because they often are thinking of demands rather than gathering information. This further shifts the process to thinking rather than reacting emotionally.

Making your agenda: You can briefly mention that they will be making their agenda with your assistance. You will be asking them each for a list of proposed topics to discuss today and then helping them agree on the order to address them, at least the first topic or two.

Making your proposals: You can briefly mention that they will be making proposals on the issues that they have raised in their agenda. You will give them a simple, 3-step process of making proposals, asking questions about each of their proposals, then responding with "Yes." "No." Or: "I'll think about it." It keeps it simple and focused. You will explain it in more depth when it comes to the third stage of the process: Making Your Proposals.

Making your decisions: Finalizing their decisions is often hard for high conflict people. Let them know that their agreements really are up to them and that you are not pressuring them to make agreements. Tell them that you will let them know about details they might not have thought of, so that they can address everything possible and put them into their final agreement, so that they can stick with their decisions once they have made them.

Emphasize the Future

Repeat and repeat that the focus will be on the future throughout this process.

> *"Our focus in this mediation is on the future and what to do going forward. There will be very little discussion of the past. I actually can't mediate the past, so we'll be looking at your proposals for the future. You don't have to agree on what happened in the past. You don't have to defend the past. And I don't need to know the past. You each know the past from your point of view, which you can keep in mind when making your proposals for your future agreements and plans."*

A little is okay: Keep in mind that you may need to talk a little about the past for information that will help in planning the details about the future. That is why it's better to say there will be *little discussion* of the past rather than *no discussion*. If the mediation heads into the past and the discussion is manageable, that's okay. But if it breaks down in blame and defensiveness, you can simply bring them back to the future. "Let's come back to discussing what to do going forward about this. Remember, we're focusing on the future here."

Safety issues: One exception to the idea that you don't need to know the past facts of the case is safety issues. It is generally best to find this out before you are meeting together with the parties. For example, having a separate Pre-Mediation Coaching or screening session is important in separation and divorce cases where there may have been domestic violence. You're not going to be able to figure this out when they are sitting in front of each other or viewing each other on the screen. There is a full discussion of the issue of Pre-Mediation Coaching later in this book in Chapter 12.

Mediation briefs: Some mediations, such as those involving civil litigation with lawyers, may require the parties to submit mediation briefs prior to the mediation. Read those and then when you start the mediation itself tell them you have read them so that there is no need to repeat what is there. When they are together, you don't want to open up the past much if you can avoid it.

Signing Paperwork

At this point, if there is an Agreement to Mediate that needs signing by the parties, go ahead with that. If payment needs to be made, take care of this. Some mediation services do not have fees or forms, so this may be not be an issue at all. Be aware that even these formalities can become a sticking point for some high conflict people. Make it a decision for the parties to make, with proposals offered by each person. You might suggest three options for how to deal with whatever their dilemma is at this point. You can be patient, because they are establishing how they are going to use their skills by making these first decisions. It's good practice and your patience will often inspire them to work harder, since they will see that you are not going to make these decisions for them.

Dealing with Resistance

Throughout each stage of the *New Ways for Mediation* process you will get resistance if you are working with one or more high conflict people. Issues will pop up that surprise you because no one else has had any problem with that particular issue. With high conflict people, often *the issue's not the issue; the personality is the issue.* So, don't get rattled. Instead use EAR statements and educate them on the *issue* they are raising.

> *"I can understand your concern about not wanting to sign the Agreement to Mediate without reviewing it with an attorney. You may not realize that this is not about the decisions you will be making regarding your dispute. It is actually only about my ability to work with you.*
>
> *"It's like signing a contract to work with a plumber at your house when you have a leak. It's necessary to have it signed in advance in order to get the work done. You will not have to make any big decisions today, without reviewing them with an attorney. But our firm does not allow me to proceed without*

this signed; that's why it was sent out to you a week ago. So, it's up to you. We, of course, will need to charge the one-hour non-refundable fee. So, you might want to just get started with gathering some information and having some initial discussions for this hour, by signing this now and taking it with you to an attorney afterward."

The same type of problem may come up about payment for the mediation. The same EAR-and-Educate approach will help.

Conclusion

This first stage of the mediation process really does set the stage for managing a high conflict mediation. By asserting the mediator's role and control from the start, it will make it much easier to manage upsets and stalemates later on.

CHAPTER 8

Stage 2: Making Their Agenda

M aking their agenda involves two main steps:

1. getting their initial thoughts and questions about the decisions they need to make, then
2. deciding the topics and order for their agenda.

Avoid Open-Ended Opening Statements

In the *New Ways for Mediation* method we don't ask for an Opening Statement by each party. Instead, we briefly ask for their initial thoughts and questions about the decisions they are facing. This is a dramatic shift from normal mediations in which the opening statement is an important part of starting the mediation. Giving the clients a chance for *feeling heard* and *getting it off their chests* has always been valued by mediators. However, with high conflict mediations this is often where the mediation falls apart. Here's why:

Preoccupation with the Past: People with high conflict personalities tend to be preoccupied with the past—defending their own past behavior (which is often a significant part of the problem) and intensely blaming others involved in the dispute (who may or may not have contributed to the problem at all—since some high conflict cases involve only one HCP and others have two or more HCPs). Ironically, giving them an uninterrupted opportunity to tell their stories reinforces staying in the past and avoiding responsibility for the future—whether the story is about what happened yesterday, last month or years ago.

Intense negative emotions: As we described in Chapter 3, high conflict people (HCPs) chronically feel helpless, vulnerable, weak and like a victim-in-life because they generally aren't able to go through the five stages of the grieving and healing process, just staying stuck in the anger stage. Even when meeting with each party separately, this storytelling can shut down openness to change and creativity in finding solutions. This reinforces staying stuck in crisis emotions which makes it harder for the brain to engage in logical, future-focused problem-solving. That's why one of the Fuhgeddaboudits is steering them clear of their negative emotions as much as possible.

Triggering the other party: Another reason for avoiding such open-ended statements is that HCPs tend to tell the story of how rotten the other person is for what they have done in the past and how upset it makes them. In joint mediations, they are doing this in front of the other person, which tends to trigger their upset emotions as well. Their emotions can also be self-stimulating, such that some HCPs seem to get a *high* from telling their stories in front of the other party, just as addicts get a *high* from telling stories of their past experiences using drugs.

Not moving forward: HCPs constantly get stuck in their stories and repeat them over and over again to whomever will listen—especially people they perceive as being in positions of authority who may become advocates for their viewpoint. Such *negative advocates* are usually hooked by the HCP's emotions, rather than their information, and most HCPs have experienced the success of this emotional storytelling—at least in the short-term until their negative advocates abandon them after becoming more informed.

Avoiding responsibility for problem-solving: In addition to trying to persuade dispute resolvers to become negative advocates with their storytelling, HCPs also reinforce their own chronic sense of helplessness by telling their stories. This is usually the outcome of their stories: "Now you see why I feel like such a helpless victim—there's nothing that I can do." This theme of helplessness appears to relieve them of all responsibility for problem-solving.

The stories also tend to place 100% of the responsibility on others—especially the other party or parties to the dispute—including prior dispute resolvers, including their complaints about prior lawyers, mediators, judges, and others. By the end of the story, they hope that you will be persuaded:

A. That they have no responsibility for the problem
   or the solution
B. That the other party is totally the source of the problem
C. That you are the only one who can help them

Often, the result of hearing this intense storytelling process is that you, as the dispute resolver, feel stressed, angry and/or helpless, and eager to get the case over, instead of eager to help them solve problems.

Initial Thoughts and Questions

Avoid anything that opens up the past, unmanaged emotions, and pressure on you to take sides. We have found that the best way to do this is to ask them a narrow *thinking* question about the present as a replacement for an opening statement:

> *"Briefly, tell me your initial thoughts and questions about the decisions you need to make today. Then we will make your agenda."*

Or simply:

> *"Do you have any questions about the decisions you need to make today, before we make your agenda?"*

This gives each party a turn to speak, without getting deep into the case. This can be brief. Long statements with high conflict people usually lead to trouble. Instead, this gives you a chance to answer their questions, show empathy for their concerns (EAR Statements), and get an idea of where they are headed in the mediation.

Suggesting questions: Depending on the type of mediation you are providing, you may even suggest some questions they may want to ask.

> *"You may wonder if an agreement needs to be written up, whether anyone needs to approve it after you are done, whether anything will be filed with a court. Let me know."*

If the mediation is in the context of a pre-existing set of issues, you could suggest that they address thoughts and questions about those issues. For example, in a divorce mediation case without lawyers involved, you might say:

"Please make sure to let me know your thoughts and questions in at least these five areas: parenting plan, child support, alimony, property division, and any timing issues, such as deadlines coming or planned moves or house sales. I will give you some brief background information in each area. I encourage you each to consult with separate lawyers, counselors, and financial advisors for more detailed information and advice."

"You don't have to have anything figured out yet. This just lets me know where you are starting from in terms of information needed for making your decisions."

Who goes first? Throughout potentially high conflict mediation, it helps to keep the burden of deciding who goes first on the parties. By making lots of these little process decisions throughout the mediation, it keeps them thinking and making joint decisions, and not relying on you to fix everything for them (which HCPs often try to do). This will help them build toward the bigger joint decisions.

Be stricter about interruptions: In normal mediations, little interruptions sometimes lead to productive discussions. In high conflict mediations, one or both parties may have trouble listening without interrupting the other. You will need to nip this in the bud sooner, so that they don't just suddenly escalate their emotions in response to being interrupted and have difficulty calming down again. Use your EAR Statements to re-direct them to listening and taking turns. Of course, as with any mediation, you can suggest taking brief notes while they are listening to help avoid interrupting.

Little negative side comments: Throughout high conflict mediation, HCPs often make little negative comments (or faces) about what each other has said. "She's no good at math." "He'll never understand this." In general, it's best to simply ignore these comments. By confronting them, you appear to have taken sides and you may end up getting side-tracked down a rabbit hole as the commenter gets defensive or denies making a comment or a face.

However, sometimes the other client may turn to you and say: "Make her stop commenting." Or: "What are you going to do about what he just said?" In this case, you have to do something. We suggest that you address both of them by looking back and forth as you say something like this:

"Listen, folks. Let's all of us try not to make little side comments and let's all of us try not to react to little side comments. Now, where were we?"

This way you are not singling out one party and seeming to take sides. If side comments persist as a serious issue, then it may be time for a caucus with each of the parties separately.

Answer their questions: Once you have heard their initial thoughts and questions from both of them, answer them as best as you can. This is a chance to reinforce the tone of the mediation as one of them asking and you answering questions in the search for useful information for making their proposals and decisions.

Building Their Agenda

Once you have answered all of the questions that you can, it is time for making their agenda. Here are some steps you can use to do that.

Ask for proposed topics: You can ask both of the parties for their proposed lists of topics:

"Who would like to go first in telling us your list of proposed agenda items?"

This is another little joint decision for them to make. Write down their list as they are saying it, without comment or judgement. Then write down the other client's list.

Get agreement on topics and order: Before you ask them to put their topics in order, suggest to them that it often helps to start with little topics first to build momentum for big topics later. But also let them know it's up to them.

Then ask them which topic they would like to start with. Then the next and the next. You may not need to make a very long list if there are only one or two topics that they came to discuss.

Clarify reality about topics: They may pick the biggest, most difficult topic to start with. They often do this because they are so anxious about it or it truly needs to be established to make their other decisions. For example, in a divorce case, it may be which parent is going to have the majority of the time or who is going to get the house. If this happens, suggest that they put a time limit on it so that they can get to the other topics if they are unable to reach an agreement in the expected time.

You will manage their agenda: Now that they have determined the agenda, the mediator is in charge of managing it. By referring back to it regularly as their agenda, you strengthen their sense of responsibility and focus.

Changing topics later: Keep in mind that it is very common for high conflict people to go off their agenda. They add new issues and make the discussion larger and larger in an effort to *win* on an issue. This makes things worse, not better, of course. In this situation, you can just gently remind them of their agenda item and ask if they want to add the additional items later to the agenda. If they insist on a new topic in the moment, ask them if they want to change their agenda to the new topic now. If so, it's up to them, but get them to make it a *decision* to switch topics rather than an *impulse*. This keeps you in a very neutral position, because you are managing *their* agenda rather than defending your own. It is such a common problem in high conflict cases that the mediator ends up in a tug of war over his or her agenda, and this is how to manage that.

For example, the mediation may be about a construction defect. The topic is a persistent leak in the second-floor bathroom, but suddenly the customer is talking about faulty floorboards in the living room, in an effort to prove that the contractor was negligent throughout the house. The mediator can say (similar to Chapter 6 regarding Making the Agenda):

> *"Now you were talking about the bathroom leak issue, but you just started bringing up a living room floorboard issue. Both of these can be important. So, do you want to stick with your agenda item and save this for later, or switch to this new topic now? It's up to the two of you."*

This way, the mediator remains neutral about which topic to discuss and the parties have to make another joint decision. This reinforces how this method is designed to focus entirely on the process and not the outcome. It makes the clients think and work together, even in small ways.

Conclusion

This chapter has explained the importance of having potentially high conflict clients play a bigger role in the process of gathering information and making their agenda. This makes them think and gain skills and a sense of responsibility for making progress.

The mediator really does act as a guide in both parts of this stage: answering *their* questions about the decisions they are facing and assisting them in creating *their* agenda. This does not need to be a belabored process, but it needs to be conscious as the potentially high conflict parties are dissuaded from negative behavior and focused on positive behavior. It is relatively easy to do this, once you have gotten used to the main principles of step-by-step guidance to help the parties use their skills.

CHAPTER 9

Stage 3: Making Their Proposals

Now that you have guided them to make their agenda, you can go straight to their proposals. Just as we do not spend time in this method on opening statements and getting background on the conflict, we also do not spend time on identifying and exploring interests before we go to proposals, as described in Chapter 8. Therefore, you may get to their proposals in just 10-30 minutes from the start of the mediation. In most cases, Stages 1 and 2 do not need to take much time at all. For those with very time-limited mediations, this approach can be very efficient for you.

But this approach may surprise most mediators who have been trained in the interest-based negotiations model. In that approach, you explore interests before discussing proposals or anything else. By the end of this chapter, you will understand how you may still deal with their interests, but in a way that is more realistic when working with high conflict people.

Ask for questions first: Once you are at the first topic in their agenda, ask if they have any questions you can answer about this topic before you hear proposals. Asking for their questions should be routine by now.

Preparing them for proposals: Now is the time to explain the proposal-making process, which you may have mentioned in Stage 1: Establishing the Process. This can be brief, as follows:

"Proposals are the building blocks of agreement. After you make proposals, ask questions which will help lead us toward new proposals and new responses until you have an agreement.

When we make proposals, we use a 3-step process, which keeps it simple:

1. *First, one of you makes a proposal, containing Who will do What, When and Where.*

2. *Then, the other asks questions about the proposal—such as when it starts, what your part is in the plan—which are also Who, What, When and Where questions.*

   Please don't ask Why questions, because those are usually criticisms in disguise. Then the proposer answers those questions.

3. *Then, the other says 'Yes,' 'No,' or 'I'll think about it.'*

This keeps it very focused on what to do, rather than talking about the past, who to blame, or other complaints. And if the responder says "No," then the responder makes a proposal. We go back and forth until we develop a good plan—an agreement.

Any questions about that?"

Who goes first? As mentioned in making their agenda, it helps to have them decide who goes first in making a proposal. Perhaps one has a proposal ready and the other does not. Perhaps one tried to announce their proposal at the start of the process and you told them to wait until now. Or they may debate a bit over who goes first. Let them decide, as this is an important part of them getting used to making joint decisions.

Tight control: As soon as the first person makes their proposal, a high conflict person will usually attack the proposal: "That's ridiculous! You know I'll say No to that proposal." Or: "Why didn't you make that proposal a year ago? We could have saved thousands of dollars!"

This is when the mediator needs to assertively interrupt and redirect them back to questions:

"Hang on a moment folks. This is when you need to ask questions about the proposal first. Remember, proposals are the building blocks of agreement. If we really understand the proposal, then we might find better terms for an agreement. For example, I have a question: When would this plan begin?"

[Or ask some other appropriate question, to demonstrate calmly asking Who, What, When and Where questions about the proposal.]

After the mediator's question is answered, turn to the other party (the responder) and instruct them to ask 1-2 questions, making sure that they are the Who, What, When, and Where type of questions. If they continue to just react emotionally without self-control, suggest a question or two that they could ask or you could ask.

Don't let them defeat you: This question-and-answer process is the core element of high conflict mediation and it may take some extra attention on the part of the mediator to help them focus on questions rather than reactions. This really forces them to think, rather than arguing. You have to keep tight control and interrupt them if they go off the tracks. Yet if you can succeed here, the whole mediation will usually be a success. The key is in re-directing them to simply make proposals and then ask their questions and provide their information.

Back and forth: When asking questions, the responder may suddenly offer an adaptation to the proposer's proposal, which is really a new proposal. This can turn into a fast back and forth over adaptations and adaptations, and questions and answers. This is okay as long as it is productive. You may find yourself needing to slow this down, which you can do by clarifying a new proposal and then asking the other party for questions about that. The fundamental concern is always: Is this productive or breaking down?

Don't get in their way: If they are going back and forth with reasonable proposals, questions, and responses in a productive manner, it's also okay to simply listen and watch—unless they get stuck or in trouble. Just remember that at any moment high conflict clients can switch back to arguing and escalating, in which case you will need to jump in to re-direct them.

Summarize, reframe or clarify: As the mediator, you can also slow down the process by interrupting to summarize a new proposal or new response, or to reframe what was said in a more positive way, or to clarify your understanding of what was said.

Responder makes proposals: Make sure that the responder

makes the next proposal if he or she has said no to a proposal. If the first proposal is accepted, then work out the details and no further proposal needs to be made. But most commonly, it takes 1-2 proposals from each party before you should assume that they are truly stuck. You want to keep them busy thinking.

If/when they get stuck: If they have each made a proposal or two, and received a "No" response each time, then you can say:

> *"Now that I've heard your proposals, it seems to me that what is important to each of you is the following: Jane, you seem particularly concerned about _____. John, you seem particularly concerned about _____. Am I correct?"*

If they have clarifications on what is important to them, acknowledge those.

Write on a board: If you have a white board or large computer screen, you can type what appears to you to be most important to each of them, making any revisions that they have told you. If you are on a virtual platform, you may be able to use the whiteboard function, so that the parties can see what you have written. Or you might try sharing your screen with a Word document that you can type on while you talk. By looking at a board or screen, it reinforces the sense that this is *us against the problem*, not me against you.

Reverse interest-based negotiations: If you have reached this point of telling them what you have observed is important to each of them, you are actually telling them their interests. As the mediator, you are able to do this type of thinking. But as potentially high conflict parties, they are usually not be able to do this. Therefore, by hearing their proposals and questions about them, you have identified interests for them, which they would have been unlikely to do because interests are insight-oriented work which usually turns into a conflict with high conflict parties. Thus, we call this *reverse interest-based negotiations*. Now you can start working with interests—if necessary.

Ask for bridge proposals: Now that you have identified what is important, you can ask them to come up with new proposals that might bridge what is important to both of them.

Avoid probing questions: In this method, we avoid probing questions and replace them with educating about options. This is because probing questions are usually an attempt to give the parties insight into themselves or to discuss the past. HCPs are often quite unaware of all the options they have for resolving their dispute. Rather than trying to lead them to insights, give them more information.

Educate about 3 options: One of the best things to do when the clients are stuck is to tell them about options and what others have done. "Let's look at your choices." You can ask if they want to know what other people have done in similar circumstances. If you can, it is best to tell them three options that others have done. This way they don't reject a single option out of hand, and they don't fight over two options, with each liking one of them. With three options, it makes them think.

Educate about negotiation strategies: If they remain stuck, you can offer them some brief explanations of negotiation strategies that others have used, such as the following:

Spilt the difference: In reality, many negotiated agreements—especially over a single dollar amount—are settled somewhere roughly in the middle of the early offers. But don't suggest this at the start, or an HCP will propose an extreme amount right at the start.

Phased-in Agreement: This has helped settle cases with monthly payment plans. One wants it to be high and the other low. You can suggest that they start near one party's proposed amount and phase in the other party's proposed amount.

Get a recommendation from an expert: This approach involves the parties hiring an expert in the subject matter of their dispute, such as a property appraiser, parenting plan consultant, construction valuation expert, damages estimator for personal injury, and so forth. Then, have the parties return to mediation with a report and negotiate from there. They might just agree on the report's recommendations, or they might refine them. This approach has also settled many cases.

View confidential bottom lines: This is a last resort that Bill has used. He has each party write down on a hidden piece of paper the farthest that the party is willing to go to settle a particular issue (usually a dollar amount). Then they fold up the papers and give them to Bill. He then views them under the table so they can't see what each other wrote. He tells them whether they are likely to resolve the disputed issue or not, depending on whether their amounts overlap.

Ironically, the amounts usually don't overlap, but after he tells them that he gives them one last chance to make a proposal: "Are either of you willing to go a little farther than you wrote down to settle this issue?" And they usually do and settle the issue. It seems that when faced with the likelihood it won't get resolved at all, they are a little more motivated.

None of these methods is guaranteed. But by educating the parties on these options, it keeps a discussion that was stuck focused on thinking and hope, rather than reacting and hopelessness, which is so common for high conflict clients. It also keeps the burden on the clients to work hard rather than to sit back and expect the mediator to fix it for them. When HCPs feel the burden of budging in order to resolve a dispute, they often can do it.

Dealing with dilemmas: Throughout the mediation process, high conflict clients often come up with dilemmas for the mediator to solve. For example, two small business partners deciding to dissolve their partnership:

Business partner #1: "I think that she is hiding money. I've looked at the books and I can't prove it. But I feel that she has found a way to hide the fact that she's skimming income and hiding it. I just don't trust her."

Business partner #2: "He is always on my back about paranoid things. I have absolutely not been skimming money. I put every penny we earn into this business, as well as my blood, sweat and tears."

#1: "Mediator, make her prove that she isn't hiding money."

#2: "Mediator, make him get off my back. He's paranoid."

What should the mediator do? Talk about the books and the money? Talk about whether he is being inappropriate? Neither! The mediator should take a situation like this and put it back on the parties' shoulders. Here's how you can do that:

"You folks have a dilemma. You, #1, might be right, that she is hiding money and you can't find it. I've had cases like that. And you, #2, might be right. I've had cases where partners have been open and honest and were falsely accused. So, the question is: How do you want to resolve this dilemma? Here are three options you might consider:

1. Do more discovery. Maybe you'll find some irregularities.

2. You could look at the finances together—perhaps with an accountant—and explain how the finances have worked and the possibility that skimming could have occurred without it being visible. You could invite the business accountant to a mediation session to explain the accounting.

3. You could accept that you may never know for sure and proceed with the mediation with the information you have.

Those are three ideas you might consider. But all of this is up to you two. People resolve dilemmas like this all the time, some one way and others another way. What ideas or proposals does this suggest for you?"

This approach keeps the problem-solving and thinking burdens on the parties. They usually resolve their cases using one or more of these various methods.

Taking a break: When all else fails, suggest taking a break. This could be for 15 minutes, or even for several weeks. Time to gather more information or get consultation helps. Just taking a break from the emotions of negotiating with a disliked other party can help. If you are out of ideas, you can tell them that. Such honesty usually gets them thinking harder, either right away during a mediation session or later at another session with a fresh start.

Negative advocates: Another way to break through impasse (the parties getting stuck) is to invite their negative advocates into the mediation process. Negative advocates are like enablers or codependents with an alcoholic or addict. They tend to reinforce the negative thoughts, feelings, and behavior of a high conflict person. HCPs are always recruiting negative advocates and even mediators feel pressure from them to take sides—which you should resist. In some of our mediations it has helped to include a client's negative advocates (of course, don't use that term with them!). Sometimes, just educating them on the issues and the standards in the mediation session tends to calm them and reduce their blind advocacy of an HCP. In some situations, the negative advocates switch and become positive advocates by encouraging an HCP to be more rational and less defensive.

Lawyers and other support people: Depending on the nature of the dispute, lawyers may already be involved. Generally, nowadays, lawyers support the mediation process and are happy to help their clients negotiate rationally. Most can be very helpful at coming up with solutions that the mediator and the parties may have never considered.

At times it may be helpful to require the parties to have lawyers in the room with them. This is especially true, if there are concerns about competency to understand the mediation process or legal issues involved. Another reason is if the parties are acting inappropriately in ways that would likely improve with a lawyer for each one present.

Of course, sometimes other support people and lawyers can make the process more difficult. In this case, it may help to have a separate caucus with the party and their lawyer or support person. Then, you can more freely discuss how they can support the process more effectively.

Conclusion

Making their proposals is the centerpiece of high conflict mediation. In some ways, it's an extremely simple process. This is how you want your clients to experience it. You want to guide them through this process, keeping them focused on making proposals and asking questions that will lead to agreements. We have offered many ways of dealing with this stage of the process.

This guiding process uses all three of the skills we have discussed for mediators:

Connecting (with EAR Statements): Use these a lot. It helps to keep them calm and open to information.

Structuring: While this process may seem rigid, it makes it easier for the mediator as well as the parties, because it is so narrowly and simply focused. Of course, you can be slightly more flexible when you have the parties under control. But when tensions and mistrust are high, this structure will help you a lot. This is one of the biggest pieces of feedback we get about this method. The structure helps.

Educating: Instead of asking brilliant probing questions, which mediators are used to doing, this process focuses on giving the parties options. There's no need for them to get more defensive than they are already by asking questions that go into the past.

During this stage of the mediation, you can offer all of your information and ideas, so long as you follow these principles of guiding them rather than trying to solve their case for them. Most of the time (but not all) this method works with high conflict clients—and any clients. We often use this approach even with parties who are not high conflict. It can actually be more efficient and none of these techniques are harmful for anyone.

CHAPTER 10

Stage 4: Making Their Decisions

When they have reached initial agreement on their decisions, the mediator should make sure to go over the details that will be necessary to implement these decisions. This may include issues that the parties have been *thinking about*.

This usually means writing up a Memorandum of Agreement, which may suffice or which may be a smaller version of a legal document which will be expanded and written up by a lawyer(s). Or it may mean writing up a workplace or neighborhood plan of action, or a detailed legal agreement to be filed with a court.

In any case, the burden is really on the mediator to make sure that the parties address all of the relevant details necessary to carry out their agreements. Use your experience to know what needs to be included. Also, ask the parties to find out what they need to know and include to uphold their agreements. See if lawyers will be involved in approving the agreement or even writing it up.

When high conflict people are involved, finalizing their decisions is often a bumpy road for the following reasons:

Still arguing: They often keep arguing about an issue even after they have settled it. Remember, they tend to live in the past and want to rehash things over and over again. "You shouldn't have done that." "No, you are the one responsible for that problem." You can gently remind them: "You have an agreement about that, so you don't need to keep arguing about that." That usually pulls them back into the present—at least for a little while.

Cognitive distortions: They tend to have cognitive distortions which affect their view of what was actually said and agreed to, such as:

all-or-nothing thinking, jumping to conclusions, emotional reasoning, mind-reading, and so forth. They are usually not out of touch with reality, but rather putting a spin on things in their perceptions. They may have honestly misunderstood what the other person agreed to or what they agreed to. Clarifications are important here, but it's also important not to over-react with frustration with them. Just matter-of-factly verify what they understood their agreements were and then fill in the details that are necessary.

Changing their minds: They frequently change their minds, often after they have left the final mediation session. It appears that the structure of mediation helps them remain rational and logical. But when they go home afterward, they may ruminate and trigger their normally upset emotions without anyone to help them calm down. With this in mind during the mediation, ask them to think about what regrets they will have afterward and look into ways to address those issues now in the mediation.

Give them some time: Since high conflict people tend to change their minds a lot, it can help to give them some time to think about their agreements before finalizing them or signing a legal settlement agreement. Sometimes this means that they come back with some changes they want to make. Let them know the rules about that relevant to the type of agreements they are making.

If the mediation was all done in a day, it is possible that lawyers or others involved may want everyone to sign any agreements before they leave. In other cases, there will be a review process involving lawyers who may have been in the mediation or were never involved. Sometimes it can take a while to get an agreement finalized, signed and sent to court. In some cases, be prepared for the process of finalizing the terms to take almost as long as the mediation process.

Buyer's remorse: High conflict people often have buyer's remorse. It can help to bring up buyer's remorse while you are finalizing the terms of agreement. Address this as something to think about while still in the mediation, to head it off afterwards.

Negative advocates: They also may have family members or friends who are upset with them for making an agreement at all with the other *side*. (That jerk!) This should also be anticipated and addressed before the parties leave mediation. Discuss the fact that the agreement belongs to the parties and others may agree or disagree, but the decisions are always up to the parties involved themselves.

Reviewing experts: These can be lawyers, accountants, and other professionals. They may know language that has to be added to sections of the agreement to make them enforceable. They may suggest changes and new proposals. Until it has been signed, these may be good ideas to bring up with the other party before they sign it. They also may say that the mediated agreement is terrible and that they could get the client a much better deal. The thing is to get all of this feedback and treat it as information to be brought back to an additional mediation session, if necessary. Otherwise, it helps to still remember that the decisions are up to the clients and not to get pushed around.

After the mediation: It's not unusual for clients to come back after a mediation wanting individual help, either with implementation of the mediated agreement or with unrelated matters. It is essential to be very clear about what your role is. If one person contacts you about undoing the agreement and the other does not want it undone, there is nothing you can ethically do for one party against the other. You must anticipate this and make this clear. It is very established in mediation ethics that a mediator cannot later serve as an advocate for either party.

In other situations, a client may want to use you for an unrelated matter. If this does not involve the other party at all, you may be able to do this. In some situations, it's best to get the other party to sign off on your doing some vaguely related work, such as for one party's relative. All of these types of issues should be clarified with a lawyer who is an expert in this area of law in your legal jurisdiction (city, state, province, etc.).

Conclusion

This final stage of the mediation process can be surprisingly complicated in high conflict cases, because of the parties' high conflict personalities. They are used to conflict without resolution, so resolution can take two to three times as long as it would in a mediation with normal clients. Just be calm and persistent and use all of the tools we have described in this section. If they want to suddenly undo all of their agreements, just approach it in a matter-of-fact manner, get their proposals for revision and help them discuss them. Or tell them why it is too late, if it truly is.

Overall, we have designed *New Ways for Mediation* around the needs of high conflict (and potentially high conflict) clients. We have practiced most of this approach in our own mediations for approximately twelve years. You should feel free to use any parts or all of it. Of course, we recommend that you get training from us or other High Conflict Institute trainers in using this model, but you are not required to.

CHAPTER 11

Tips to Help in the Process

Throughout the process of *New Ways for Mediation,* there are several tips that may help you maintain control while still assisting the parties in making their own decisions.

Have the Parties Make the Little Process Decisions

Throughout the mediation, it is best to have the little decisions—like who goes first, choosing topics, and so forth—made jointly by the parties. This helps them build a sense of cooperation that will help in making the bigger decisions. It also helps them have a sense of ownership for how the mediation goes, so that they can't blame the mediator for *making* them do anything or *not allowing* them to do anything. This reinforces that *It's up to them.*

If you think it's best to move onto another topic, ask them "Is that okay with you?" It almost always is, but this way they buy into your next steps. If they say it's not okay, then stay with the topic or tell them why they may want to consider moving on and coming back to it later. You can suggest many things, but you should ask them to approve your suggestions before moving on. If they don't agree, then see what they need to do before moving on.

Keep the Conflict Small

High conflict people tend to feel helpless, vulnerable, weak, and like a victim-in-life, so they often try to feel strong by making the dispute larger by loudly bringing in more and more issues and complaints that may or may not be related to the issue at hand. Likewise, they may have a large list of concerns that reflects their feeling of being overwhelmed. Whenever there is a question of tackling big issues or small issues, it's usually best to go with the small ones first to build momentum.

If an issue has many parts, it's often helpful to address one part at a time. If an issue is large, it can help to break it down into small parts. Explain this to the parties to help them in making their decisions about how to approach each issue. *Keep the conflict small* is an easy expression that you can use to remind them throughout the mediation process.

Acknowledge the Positives

It's easy to overlook the positive efforts and helpful comments they make, because there's so much negativity that they may have toward each other. However, if a comment includes something positive they have said about the other person, you can reinforce that. "She said you're good at closing up the office at night. That's nice." You don't need to exaggerate the value of such comments; just acknowledge them and move on.

Ignore the Little Negatives (if Possible)

HCPs have many negative or distracting little comments that they may make toward each other or you as the mediator throughout the mediation, because of their lack of impulse control. ("That's not true." "She always says things like that." "Just like a man to say that." "You're being stupid.") We recommend ignoring these little comments as much as possible. Otherwise, if you confront the commenter, they will take you *down the rabbit hole* of deny, attack, defend. Instead, keep them in the discussion of the topic at hand as if the comment never happened.

Sometimes a comment cannot be ignored. The other party may demand that it be confronted. In such a case, it's recommended to make a general announcement to all parties about future comments, rather than focusing on the commenter, such as the following scenario.

In the middle of the mediation, one party makes a mildly nasty side comment and the other party reacts with: "What are you going to do about that comment she just made, Ms. Mediator?"

The mediator says, looking at both parties: "Ok, folks. Let's all try not to make side comments and let's all try not to react to side comments. Okay? Thank you. Now, let's continue on this topic."

They almost always accept that announcement and abide by it better than before.

Don't Suggest the Negative

It is common for the parties in high conflict cases to suggest the negative from time to time (whether an HCP or exasperated party opposing an HCP). "She'll never agree to that." "He'll never accept any of my proposals." Sometimes they introduce a proposal by saying "I don't know why you won't consider doing such-and-such." It often helps to interrupt on the spot and tell that person to try taking out the negative suggestion and just make their proposal in positive terms. "I would like us to do such-and-such." This teaches them both to negotiate better.

Sometimes mediators also suggest the negative. "I know you're not going to like this, but you'll need to take XYZ policy into account if you're talking about changing this office procedure." Instead, just put it in positive terms. "Just for a heads up, you'll need to take XYZ policy into account if you're talking about changing this office procedure."

Negative Words to Avoid

In line with avoiding suggesting the negative, there are many words that tend to trigger high conflict people unnecessarily. For example: "Would you be willing to make this concession…?" It suggests the negative to people who see the world in all-or-nothing, win-lose terms. Instead, phrase it as a benefit or simply ask what their thoughts are about a proposal without giving it a label. If the following words get used by the parties, try to reframe them into more positive words. This is just a list to begin with. You can add your own.

Words and Phrases to Avoid:

concession

compromise

Can you accept…?

Can you agree to…? (This implies that you have taken sides in favor of one party's proposal.)

position (as in "Is it your position that…?")
(Reframe positions to be proposals. "Is it your proposal that…? Positions lock people in. Proposals are expected to be flexible.)

discovery (While mediation can be viewed as a process for discovering good solutions, many clients just think of the legal term "discovery" and having to produce records)

justice, truth, fairness (These wrongly imply that such personal values issues can get resolved in mediation. High conflict people use these terms a lot, but they cannot be mediated. Remember: Keep the conflict small)

trust (This is another big personal value that cannot be mediated. But there are thousands of little types of trust behaviors: "I trust you will drive safely with the children, but I don't trust that you will be honest about your income, so let's set up some protections in our Agreement.")

Apology Quicksand

While apologies resolve many disputes between reasonable people, they are a much different matter with HCPs and usually need to be avoided. However, don't be surprised that high conflict people frequently will demand an apology from another party, at times saying that they cannot move forward without such an apology. Sometimes a reasonable person will demand an apology from a high conflict person because of their extreme behavior, also saying that they can't move forward without it. Many mediations bog down here in the apology quicksand.

For many HCPs, demanding an apology is a move to dominate or humiliate the other party, and to justify their own behavior. HCPs tend to live in the past, trying to re-write history to blame the other party completely for anything that has gone wrong. Therefore, their request for an apology is often not appropriate at all because the other party has done nothing wrong—it just *feels* that way to the HCP. They see things in all-or-nothing terms and cannot accept any responsibility or gray areas in what has occurred. By seeking an apology, they can deny any responsibility whatsoever for the conflict, when it often is partly or mostly their own behavior that was a problem.

On the other hand, a reasonable person may seek an apology from a high conflict person because of inappropriate actions or statements that the HCP actually made. But HCPs are the last people to apologize because they see things in all-or-nothing terms and an apology would *feel like* accepting that it was all their fault.

So, regardless of who is asking for an apology, the mediator is encouraged to quickly respond and try to steer away from this issue before they get stuck in the apology quicksand. You can say something like this:

> *"Actually, apologies take us back into the past and we are trying to move forward in the present and make agreements about the future in this mediation. So, unless someone wants to apologize quickly and move on, it's usually not a productive thing to focus on. Also, I have found that apologies often drain off the energy for change, such that a person who has made an apology may feel no need to put energy into trying to change for the future. It's better to request or propose how you want things to be in the future, rather than to focus on what you didn't like in the past. That usually just gets into a big argument, without any energy left for making things better in the future. Can we agree to focus forward now on the Agenda items?"*

Writing Lists

A surprisingly simple and often helpful tool in high conflict mediation (or any mediation) is to have the parties write lists in the middle of the process. This can be useful if they are stuck on issues or emotions. This can often help calm the parties, as writing tends to shift people from their right-brain defensiveness to their left-brain problem-solving. The list can be specific to the problem at hand.

For example, in a child custody mediation they could both write down a list of holidays that are important to each of them, to help determine which parent the child would be with each holiday over the course of the years. Many custody mediators simply figure this out for the parties, but with high conflict parties it tends to help them work together by making this a productive joint task, since it isn't that complicated and is focused on the future.

> **A couple:** *In a heated mediation regarding the break-up of a 20-year relationship, the parties were stuck in angry arguments over whether they should split up or not, and whose*

fault it was. Talking about the relationship and their feelings went nowhere. They had been in couples counseling with no resolution. The mediator suggested that sometimes it helps to make lists of what would need to be divided up between them if they separated. "Sometimes this helps couples decide not to split up because they realize the full impact of such a decision. And sometimes this helps them realize that they do want to go ahead and part ways, and it focuses them more calmly on what decisions need to be made."

When the parties returned for a second mediation session a week later, they were calmer and had decided that they would split up. They had each made pages of lists of furniture (some of it quite expensive) which they would need to divide up, much of it purchased on many trips around the world. ("I bought that armoire in France. No, we bought it together in Spain." "Oh, you're right. Now I remember.") By focusing on their lists and objective details over the next six sessions (two hours each), they were able to reach a full agreement while also recognizing the positive experiences they had enjoyed together over the years.

A business partnership: *Two women shared a business that involved putting on educational programs. Things had recently blown up between them which included one locking the other out of the office by changing the locks. The other filed a court case. Yet when they came to mediation, one wanted to repair their working relationship and the other wanted to end it. With little progress made over several hours, the mediator suggested that they both write two lists and meet again in mediation the following week. The two lists were:*

1. *Assume that you maintain the partnership. What steps would you have to take to make it work?*

2. *Assume that you end the partnership. What steps would you have to take to wind down the partnership, including dividing its assets, client lists, and your financial interests in it?*

Both partners were to write both lists, to help them decide which way they wanted to go.

The following week, they came to mediation agreeing to terminate the partnership, but to put on one more program together. The tension from the prior week seemed to have totally dissipated allowing the mediation to focus on the big issues and they agreed to work out the smaller issues on their own.

Challenging the Mediator

High conflict people tend to view all relationships as adversarial, so don't be surprised if you are verbally attacked by one or more parties during the process. This does not happen a lot, but it can happen occasionally in some cases. Do not take this personally, as it's a blaming issue that HCPs have and not about your competence, even though they say that it is. If they really feel that you are incompetent, they will fire you rather than argue with you. Instead, some HCPs want to make the mediator feel as bad as they do. So, they may criticize you or say that you're not helping.

In these situations, just put the burden back on the clients. Then ask what they are proposing should be done? Do they want to go to the next topic? Do they have something else they think would be more helpful to do? Avoid getting defensive and just treat it as another problem to solve.

They may challenge the way you are managing the mediation, perhaps because they have been in another mediation that focused more on the past or feelings. Just emphasize that this is the way you work and that you believe that you will be most helpful to them by taking this approach.

Gender, Age, or Ethnic Challenges of the Mediator

Sometimes a high conflict person will challenge the mediator because of their gender, age, or racial/ethnic background. It may be simply another form of challenging the mediator to gain influence over the mediator or to make the mediator feel as bad as they do.

However, if it is a serious challenge to you being their mediator, you can say that they are here already and this is how you work and can help them. If they are uncomfortable with your process or role, they can seek a different mediator. It's really up to them. Don't get into power struggles with HCPs. "This is who I am and this is how I work. You're already here. Shall we begin? It's up to you."

High Conflict Lawyers

Lawyers make up a substantial percentage of those who also perform mediations nowadays. They also have been participating in mediations with their clients for decades. On the whole, lawyers have been very helpful in legal mediations because they are able to assist the parties in coming up with creative proposals and to assist the mediator in addressing the details of agreements which otherwise might have been overlooked. In fact, many court systems are requiring mediation as an early step in legal disputes now, more than ever before.

However, with the apparent increase in personality disorders and high conflict personalities in society, we are also seeing more high conflict lawyers in mediation. Some of the ways to manage such lawyers are to use the same tips and strategies with them that you would use with high conflict clients. It's their personality, not their position, that drives their behavior.

You can give them EAR Statements ("I know this can be frustrating, but it usually works"), talk about choices ("I can meet with you separately or jointly"), and set limits by referring to rules and standards that they must follow ("Remember, we are all expected to seriously pursue settlement in good faith.") Some jurisdictions have civility standards for lawyers, such as California which includes the following regarding alternative dispute resolution, such as mediation:

> An attorney should use an alternative dispute resolution process for purposes of settlement and not for delay or other improper purposes, such as discovery.

> An attorney should participate in good faith, and assist the alternative dispute officer [mediator] by providing pertinent and accurate facts, law, theories, opinions and arguments in an attempt to resolve a dispute.
> ....
> In family law proceedings an attorney should seek to reduce emotional tension and trauma and encourage the parties and

attorneys to interact in a cooperative atmosphere, and keep the best interest of the children in mind.[11]

Perhaps such standards could be posted in a mediation room. A mediator can also meet in caucus with each party and their lawyer, or with just the lawyers, or in some cases with just the parties (with the lawyers' agreement). It can be helpful to say from the start that these combinations are all possible and that the mediator may suggest them at times during the mediation process, and that the parties or their attorneys may request them at any time.

Some mediators start out the process by meeting with the lawyers together without their clients, just to set the stage for a productive mediation. If there is a possible high conflict lawyer, this gives an opportunity for the mediator to set expectations and limits, as well as to help decide whether to do a shuttle mediation rather than a joint mediation.

Conclusion

These tips can be applied at any time in any mediation, and especially as needed during a mediation with high conflict participants. They all follow the theme of helping clients stay focused on logical problem solving, rather than emotional reactions. They also tend to be counter-intuitive, so it helps to remind yourself of these occasionally to avoid accidently getting hooked into a high conflict discussion that will blow up.

CHAPTER 12

Pre-Mediation Coaching

It often takes high conflict people quite a while to make progress in mediation, because they often have to process everything twice: once in their emotional reactions to upsetting information and new ideas, then again to calm down and really think about things logically in a problem-solving manner with the help of the mediator. It can take them twice as long or longer to reach agreements compared to non-HCPs.

It is not unusual for them to fail to reach an agreement on the issues in their first mediation session and sometimes this failure turns them off to trying mediation again. With all of this in mind, pre-mediation coaching can help increase the likelihood that they will reach an agreement in mediation, even in their first session.

(For coaching specific to workplace disputes, see brief description of *New Ways for Work*SM *Coaching* in Chapter 11: Pre-Mediation Programs, and more detailed discussion within Chapter 12: Workplace Issues.)

Goals of Pre-Mediation Coaching

There are at least three goals for a Pre-Mediation Coaching session, which can each be considered steps in the coaching session:

1. Explain the process and teach them the skills they should use during the mediation.
2. Hear the client's biggest concerns and expected toughest issues.
3. Screen for appropriateness for mediation, including power imbalance issues.

Throughout the coaching you can emphasize building rapport and showing empathy, attention and respect for their concerns. Since the other party is not present, you can be more flexible about hearing about the past and allowing emotions, but do not open up too much because it is still important to emphasize that the mediation will focus on the future and problem-solving.

Structuring the Coaching Session

This should be a separate session with each party, not together. Typically, the coaching session can be about an hour and ideally scheduled a week or two before the mediation session, so it will be fairly fresh for the client. Ideally, this will be in person or virtual face-to-face, but sometimes it may need to be over the phone. In some cases, at the mediation itself, the mediator may meet with each party separately for a few minutes of coaching before starting the joint mediation process.

The coach for the Pre-Mediation Coaching can be the mediator or someone else, such as a counselor, a lawyer, or a staff person for the mediator. It can be the same person for each or a different person for each. In some cities there are counselors or divorce coaches who make pre-mediation coaching a specialty part of their practices. However, most commonly it is the mediator who does this Pre-Mediation Coaching with each party in preparation for the mediation with the same mediator. For a mediator, it gives you an opportunity to build a good connection with each, to get a sense of what each person will be like during the mediation, and to discuss issues they may not be comfortable addressing in front of the other party.

To focus the discussion, you can give them a handout such as the 2-page *Client Mediation Handout* in Appendix B, or the *New Ways for Families—Pre-Mediation Coaching Workbook* or the *New Ways for Work Coaching Workbook,* both available at **www.HighConflictInstitute.com.**

Goal #1: Explain Process and Skills

You can start a coaching session with brief chit-chat, but don't discuss the case until you have explained the mediation process and the 4 Big Skills™ described below. Avoid the temptation to start with them telling you their story. Remember, the bigger problem for HCPs is lack of self-restraint, not lack of self-expression. Help them restrain themselves by listening first to you describing the mediation process and teaching them the skills they will need to use in the process. Many mediators get this backwards, but you will have more control and confidence if you hold off on any storytelling and make the process the first priority.

In explaining the mediation process, emphasize the mediator's role as guiding the process and answering questions, while the clients will just have four simple tasks: asking questions, making their agenda (with your guidance), making their proposals (with your guidance), and making their decisions. Emphasize that the focus will be on the future rather than the past.

Then teach them the 4 Big Skills, focusing on the 2-page handout or pre-mediation coaching workbook, as follows:

1. Managed emotions: Learning this skill can help you stay calm when so-and-so is talking in the mediation. It will help you appear reasonable and focused on solutions. Discuss the idea of your client creating a self-soothing phrase that he or she can use to stay calm throughout the process.

2. Flexible thinking: This can help you resolve your dispute in a way that works for you. Think of one or two proposals you can make during the mediation for each item you want to put on the agenda. This can make the mediation more efficient and less likely to get stuck in talking about the past and who did what to whom.

Teach the 3-step proposal making process:

Step 1: **Make a proposal:** This usually will include WHO will do WHAT, WHEN and WHERE.

Step 2: **Ask questions:** When would this begin? What would my part be? Can you give me a detailed picture of how you see this working? Then the proposer answers the questions. The mediator can also ask questions.

Step 3: **Respond:** Simply say "Yes." "No." Or "I'll think about it." If Yes, then "We can write it up." If No, then calmly say you disagree, and focus on making a new proposal. Both people need to make proposals, so both people are thinking of ideas. If it is "I'll think about it," then find out how long they need to think or agree on a time limit.

3. Moderate behavior: By being moderate in your behavior, you are less likely to trigger defensiveness in the other party. This will help both of you stay focused forward on problem-solving rather slipping back into emotions and arguments.

Some examples of moderate behavior (included in the client handout) are:

A. Don't interrupt while the other person is speaking. Instead, make notes to remind yourself of any ideas that pop up while he or she is talking. Then you can raise them when appropriate.

B. Treat everyone with respect. This means avoiding insulting comments, raising your voice or pointing fingers. These behaviors often trigger defensiveness in the other person. Instead, you want everyone to stay calm and rational, in order to focus on solving the problems you came to discuss. Speaking respectfully goes a long way toward reaching agreements that will work and last over time.

C. Use "I" statements. These are sentences that start with "I feel…" or "I prefer…" or "I have another idea…" Avoid "You" statements, such as "You always…" or "You never…" "You" statements tend to trigger defensiveness in the other person, which will make it harder to reach an agreement. Just use "I" statements to convey your own perspective, rather than assumptions or criticisms of the other person's perspective. Remember, all you need to do is to reach an agreement. You don't need to try to change the other person's way of thinking (which is unlikely anyway).

D. Ask to take a break, if necessary. Avoid just getting up and walking out. Ask for a break, so that everyone can stop for a few minutes. Mediation is more flexible than a court hearing or arbitration. Taking breaks can help you earn respect—rather than resentment if you rush out—and can help you calm down if you're upset. It's also fine to take a break to get advice from a lawyer, friend or other advisor before you make final agreements. Just ask for some time to do so—either a few minutes, or several days or weeks if necessary. Mediators generally do not pressure you to make final decisions at the same time as you first discuss an issue.

4. Check yourself: Check from time to time to see if you are using these skills before, during, and after the mediation.

Explain each skill by saying how it can benefit the client. For example:

1. Managed emotions: Learning this skill can help you stay calm when so-and-so is talking in the mediation. It will help you appear reasonable and focused on solutions.

2. Flexible thinking: This can help resolve your dispute in a way that works for you, by making proposals and being open to new ideas and proposals.

3. Moderate behavior: It can be really helpful to communicate in ways that don't trigger the other person's defensiveness. Most people don't think about their influence on the other person when they are upset, but you can influence them in either a negative or positive direction by your own behavior.

4. Check yourself: Regularly ask yourself if you are using these skills before, during and after the mediation.

Practicing with the Client

If it seems appropriate, you can practice at least one example of one of these skills in a role-play exercise with the client. Suggest that the client take the role of the Other Party in the dispute for a minute or two, and you can play the Client. For example, the client may be an employee in a mediation with his/her manager. Ask the client (playing the Other Party, the manager) to say something the Other Party might say in the mediation that would be upsetting for the client. Then, you (playing the Client, the employee) respond using one of the skills. For example:

Client as Manager says:	You're not getting enough work done! You're always slow!
Coach as Employee says:	(Remembering not to take it personally): Then I have a proposal: Why don't you tell me what your priorities are, since you have several projects for me?

Then, switch roles and you be the Other Party and let the Client play himself or herself. Repeat the exercise. Clients often find this very helpful, because they didn't have the words and just got upset in the past. If you have time, you can do several such exercises or you can let the client talk about other issues.

Goal #2: Hearing the Client

Once you've laid the groundwork of explaining the mediation process and the skills the client should use during the process, *then* you can listen to the client's concerns and difficult issues. This puts working hard in the mediation process and using the 4 Big Skills as higher priorities than the clients' storytelling and emotions. This is important to manage with high conflict people. It is also important to keep this focused on decision-making, not open-ended storytelling about the past. However, in this private meeting you can allow for some discussion of the past.

For example:

- *What do you want me to know before we all meet together?*
- *What do you want me to know about the other party?*
- *What will be some of the hardest issues to discuss and negotiate?*
- *How will you feel discussing and negotiating issues with the other party in the room?*
- *Anything else you want me to know before we meet together?*

Coaching Tips

Throughout this discussion, you can be quite flexible depending on what you see as important. You can also coach the client on how they can apply the above skills as they discuss these issues. For example, if the client is unsure about how to handle an issue and wants your advice, you could re-direct the client like this: "You can ask questions about that issue before we make the Agenda so that both of you hear the answers about how it is commonly handled. That way I'm not giving you special information separately on any issue until you are both together."

Perhaps the client is nervous about staying calm when meeting with someone they haven't seen for a while or they are facing two or three people on the other *side* of an issue. You can coach the client to think of an encouraging statement before the mediation to tell himself or herself to help get through the mediation. We have received feedback from clients in situations like this that they found it very helpful to think of and use an encouraging statement like that.

Goal #3: Screening for Appropriateness

In some cases, such as in divorce mediation, there are concerns about power imbalances, such as understanding of financial issues, and even domestic violence. A pre-mediation coaching session is one way to assess these concerns, without making it seem like you are interrogating your clients or assuming that they are having a problem that they may not have. However, up to fifty percent of divorce cases in court have allegations of domestic violence, so it is important to address these concerns before putting the parties in the same room (or even together on the same video screen).

One tool for screening for intimate partner violence (domestic violence) in a mediation is the MASIC: Mediator's Assessment of Safety Issues and Concerns, developed by Amy Holtzworth-Munroe, Connie J. A. Beck, and Amy G. Applegate.[12] This tool can help the mediator decide whether to proceed with a mediation and, if so, what precautionary measures may be necessary to ensure a safe process.

Recently, these authors and others published a study comparing shuttle in-person mediation with litigation and videoconferencing mediation. The result was that mediators and clients slightly favored shuttle mediation over videoconferencing over litigation.[13] The implications of this for mediators, especially with the increased use of videoconferencing, is that clients and mediators may prefer to use virtual breakout rooms so that the parties do not need to see each other during the mediation. The option of not being face-to-face on the video screen should be discussed with each party during their pre-mediation coaching session.

Ask the Client to Summarize

At the end of the Coaching session, ask the client to summarize what he or she has learned. This helps the client remember better and shows how important you believe these skills are for his or her success. This also gives you an opportunity to clarify anything that the client seems to have misunderstood.

Conclusion

Pre-mediation coaching is more important in potentially high conflict mediation than in ordinary mediation, because of the risks of high conflict behavior during and after the mediation. Yet it also can help calm a client and prepare them for greater success in reaching agreements. The main caution for the coach is to avoid engaging too deeply in the client's story, venting, and blaming of the other party. It is essential to focus the client's attention primarily on the skills and tasks that they need to engage in to make the mediation a success.

CHAPTER 13

Pre-Mediation Programs

Unlike single-session pre-mediation coaching, a program provides more opportunity for practice and repetition of skills. This can be helpful with high conflict people who can learn the skills, but often take more time to absorb them.

Two programs with several sessions of skills training that High Conflict Institute has developed are *New Ways for Families*® and *New Ways for Work*® Coaching. While these can be stand-alone conflict resolution skills training programs without mediation, they also provide good preparation for successful mediations. They both emphasize the same 4 Big Skills that we have mentioned in Pre-Mediation Coaching:

1. Managed Emotions
2. Flexible Thinking
3. Moderate Behavior
4. Checking Yourself

New Ways for Families®

This is a skills training program for both parents going through a separation or divorce. There are several models of this method:

Counseling: This involves 6 Individual Parent Sessions for each parent with their own counselor, guided by a workbook. Then, there are 3 Parent-Child Sessions with a Parent-Child Counselor, also guided by the workbook. The parents never need to be together during this counseling process, so it is able to address domestic violence, parental alienation, and other high conflict issues. But the focus is on each parent learning the 4 Big Skills, so that they can then make their own agreements in mediation and implement them afterward.

Counselors need a two-day training from High Conflict Institute. At this time, counselors in over 30 cities in the United States and Canada have been trained in this model. Judges in over a dozen cities have ordered parents to receive *New Ways for Families* counseling. Parents can also voluntarily sign up for this by choosing counselors in their state or province from the list of trained counselors on the High Conflict Institute website: **www.HighConflictInstitute.com.**

Online Course: High Conflict Institute has developed a 12-unit (approximately one hour per unit) online course which teaches the same 4 Big Skills, focusing in-depth on a wide range of co-parenting issues. Thousands of parents have already been ordered to take this online course, also known as *Parenting Without Conflict by New Ways for Families,* which is readily available at **www.HighConflictInstitute. com.** Parents can also take this class voluntarily at **www.ConflictPlaybook.com,** which is our website for individuals looking to voluntarily improve their own skills. There is also a 4-unit online Parent-Child course to help parents teach their children the 4 Big Skills of New Ways for Families.

Coaching with the Online Program: High Conflict Institute is now training coaches to assist parents who are taking the online program, by answering any questions they may have, discussing their writing exercises contained within the online program, and doing role-play exercises with the coach to reinforce the skills they are learning. Typically, a parent would take three coaching sessions along with the 12-session course, but six or twelve coaching sessions are also possible.

Benefits

After parents have taken these courses, they are well-prepared for making agreements in mediation by managing their emotions, making proposals (flexible thinking), and using moderate behavior. They are also more likely to implement their agreements and make new agreements in the future on their own.

If parents live in two different states or provinces after separating, they can learn these skills where they are and then make agreements together online or in-person in mediation. This is appealing to court systems who often have to deal with cases in which one parent has moved away to another jurisdiction. With the online course, combined with coaches trained in this method across the United States and Canada, separated and divorced parents can be more cooperative and successful in mediating their co-parenting issues wherever they are located.

New Ways for Work™ Coaching

This coaching program is designed for employees and managers who may have engaged in high conflict behavior, but their organizations want to see if they can learn enough conflict resolution skills to remain employed. This method also uses a workbook and teaches the same 4 Big Skills, with a coach trained in the method. It is designed for 3 – 8 individual sessions, which could be implemented by an Employee Assistance Professional (EAP), outside counselor, or coach within the organization.

There may have been a dispute between co-workers, a manager and an employee, or even professional colleagues which could benefit from mediation. Rather than just having the disputing parties go right into mediation, it is preferable to have one or both parties get some *New Ways for Work* coaching first. Then, a manager can interview each employee to see what they have learned and find out if it is realistic to have them meet together in mediation.

For example, if one employee says: "I'm working on managing my emotions when I disagree with the other employee;" and the other says "I'm working on using flexible thinking in coming up with solutions to team problems," then a mediation may be successful. If they still blame the other for everything, then a mediation may be pointless and other decisions may have to be made.

For more on *New Ways for Work Coaching,* see the section with that title in Chapter 14: Workplace Mediation Issues.

Conclusion

Both of these programs are flexible and can be adapted to meet the needs of a family court system, a particular workplace, or other settings. By coaching individuals in using these simple conflict resolution skills, it can help them both to focus on win-win solutions rather than high conflict behavior in a mediation. However, we have found that it is best to move quickly into mediation after having learned the 4 Big Skills in these programs, as they do seem to fade if they are not applied on a regular basis.

SECTION 3

Special Issues

While high conflict personalities often have similar problems in many situations (blaming, all-or-nothing thinking, unmanaged emotions and extreme behavior), the way they can be handled in mediation varies by the environment. This section presents a full range of mediation settings, from workplace conflicts, to divorce cases, to group situations (such as elder care issues), and large group facilitation (such as public meetings). Also addressed are ethical issues and difficult endings, which occur more frequently when high conflict people are involved.

CHAPTER 14

Workplace Mediation Issues

Workplace issues present a unique set of challenges for mediators and are more complex than many mediators and employers realize, particularly with high conflict people (HCPs). We have seen mediators conduct short engagements, perhaps one joint session lasting 2-3 hours, which seems to have been effective. But then the mediator leaves and things actually end up worse. In other cases, unwary mediators have structured the process to focus on the past in an effort to clear past hurts and encourage deeper exploration, but the mediation implodes.

Workplace Issues are Different

When we are working with parties with high conflict traits, some of the challenges in mediation are:

1. **More contact:** In the workplace, the parties to a mediation will usually spend much more time working together afterward than those in most other disputes, such as divorce or civil lawsuits. Even in divorce cases, co-parents often only need to think about maintaining respectful communication with each other for 5 minutes while they hand over the kids. This workplace reality presents a significant challenge when mediating with at least one party who is an HCP.

2. **Authority concerns:** A supervisor of an employee with high conflict traits can easily end up being a target of blame, because of their position of authority over the person. This can occur even around small issues like vacation approval and work assignments, or large issues like performance feedback and managing behavior. This means there are opportunities for new conflicts every day, so

that a focus on just settling the presenting disagreements will be ineffective.

3. **Surface issues:** Parties may seem to disagree about work processes, roles and responsibilities. But when an HCP is involved, those are typically not the real issues. Instead, the HCP's emotional upset over feeling abandoned, disrespected, ignored and other personality-based concerns is the fuel for the conflict. "The issue's not the issue; the personality is the issue." (But don't say that out loud!)

4. **Co-workers:** Other co-workers are impacted, so the mediator must recognize there is a larger context with many players.

Lessons from Transformative Mediation

We cannot transform an HCP's personality in any setting. If the parties are going to continue to deal with each other in the workplace, we need to focus on a process that addresses the presenting complaint, and also help the parties build a more positive and constructive way of communicating. This requires the process to focus on helping the parties learn to apply skills in the mediation that they can take back into the workplace.

Many mediators who practice extensively in the workplace field often use the Transformative Mediation approach, which is a formal method established over the past few decades for strengthening relationships in the workplace and elsewhere. (See *The Promise of Mediation* by Robert Baruch Bush and Joseph Folger[14].) This approach can help parties change the quality of their interactions from negative and destructive to positive and constructive. "People have the capacity to regain their footing and shift back to a restored sense of strength/confidence in self (the empowerment shift) and openness/responsiveness to other (the recognition shift)."[15]

The challenge with applying this approach with HCPs is that it requires them to make shifts, which, in such a limited engagement, they are simply not capable of making. Unfortunately, when working with parties who have high conflict traits, relying on a process that encourages discussion about the past, a focus on the intention and impact of each other's behavior, and that the parties gain insight from each other, can be a recipe for failure.

The transformative model also assumes that the improvement of the interaction itself is a key goal, even more than settlement of a particular issue the parties disagree about. We agree that this is the case in workplace settings, however, we must shift our approach when working with HCPs to focus on their strengths while avoiding inadvertently triggering the parties' emotional upset and dysregulation by going into the past and focusing on gaining insight from each other.

By using the proposal-focused approach of *New Ways for Mediation*, we can aim to achieve the same objective of changing the quality of the interaction to be more positive and constructive. We skip over a focus on the past by asking parties to focus on the future. Rather than asking parties to gain insight from each other, we get them to focus on asking questions of each other and making proposals that will improve their interactions going forward.

Assessment for suitability

It is critical that the mediator needs to do an assessment for suitability of mediation prior to the mediation, which could impact whether or not to have a mediation. These concerns could include:

1. Is there *potentially* a high conflict personality involved for one or more parties?
2. Has there been a breach of standards of conduct or other behavioral breach, which should be addressed prior to the mediation?
3. Is the employer inadvertently hoping the other party will do the heavy lifting to encourage the HCP to change their behavior?
4. Does the HCP have any motivation to make behavioral changes? This could be impacted by:
   a. Fear of losing one's job
   b. Prior consequences they have received for their behavior
   c. A focus on the other party as a target of blame without taking any responsibility
   d. A focus on extreme outcomes, such as:
      i. Firing the other person
      ii. Unmanaged anger

5. Who are the advocates around the parties?
   a. Are they positive or negative advocates?
   b. Do they understand the realistic objectives of the process?
   c. Are they encouraging the parties to negotiate or to fight?

Such an assessment is very subjective, depending on all of the circumstances of the parties and of the particular dispute. When HCPs are involved, these are the types of questions that a mediator or manager should consider before proceeding with a mediation in the workplace.

Unrealistic Expectations

It is very common for one or more parties to a workplace conflict to have unrealistic expectations of mediation, especially when one or more HCPs are involved. The stress of dealing with a high conflict employee or manager often blinds people because they are so desperate to get the conflict resolved. But mediation is not a magical solution and, as mentioned above, can sometimes make things worse.

Managers: Unfortunately, managers (and union representatives) who request a mediation often do not understand the dynamics that are at play in the conflict and are unrealistic in their hopes the mediation will transform a toxic situation, particularly when an HCP is involved. Sometimes the other party feels that they are the proxy for management in being asked to participate in the mediation in hopes the HCP will *get it* and essentially make a personality shift. Also, managers very often fail to recognize their own contribution to the dynamic by not assertively setting expectations and/or addressing breaches of expected workplace behavior on a regular basis.

In an aptly-named article, "When Supervisors Refer Employees for Mediation or 'Can You Take This Mess Off My Hands?'" the authors talk about how managers often hope that the mediator can help problematic employees learn to change their behavior. They suggest that an employee's problem behavior needs to be addressed first. If it appears the supervisor knows little about what is really happening, has failed to communicate these perceptions, or failed to set appropriate limits, they suggest it is helpful to delay the mediation until the supervisor has first addressed these issues.[16]

We agree with this approach. Further, leaders who request a mediation process where there is an HCP involved need to lower their expectations and contribute to setting the criteria for success. This means appreciating the outcomes of a mediation may be to:

1. Help contain the conflict but not transform it.
2. Improve behavior and interactions but not try fixing a personality or transforming a relationship. Even a 10% improvement is still an improvement. (See "The 10% Solution" in the book *It's All Your Fault at Work*[17])
3. Return the parties to the workplace with a set of behavioral/communication agreements that the manager will play a key role in monitoring and supporting.

The Other Party: The mediator must ensure that the other party also has realistic expectations. Are they invested in wanting the HCP to gain lasting insight into their contribution to the difficulties? Will they say something that will contribute to that party's own healing? Or apologize? If so, the mediator needs to assist that party to reflect on what a more realistic goal for the process might be. If the party has realistic goals for the process, then there is a much greater potential for success.

For example, a mediation involves an HCP employee who has filed a bullying/harassment complaint against their supervisor. The supervisor acknowledges to the mediator before the mediation that the supervisor is having challenges communicating with the HCP and has gotten frustrated in the past. The supervisor sees that the HCP is having a negative impact on the workplace and sincerely wants to improve this dynamic. The supervisor realizes that the supervisor needs to improve their communication with the HCP and needs to be able to hold the HCP accountable without it devolving into further complaints and toxicity.

In this case, the supervisor has a realistic assessment of the situation, so that a mediated (or facilitated) process could be helpful. If the supervisor sees the mediation process as an opportunity to improve communication and problem-solving with the employee, then the mediation may:

1. *Effectively correct misinformation from the employee*
2. *Improve the employee's decision-making*
3. *Better engage the employee in problem-solving or help him or her handle disagreements without further complaints*
4. *Clarify the supervisor's role (very often HCPs have unrealistic expectations of supervisors)*
5. *Prevent future complaints*

With such realistic expectations, the process could be successful.

The High Conflict Party: Does the party with high conflict traits have a realistic approach to the mediation? Are they bringing issues forward that are truly negotiable? For example, if the HCP's goal is to have the other party fired, this is not something that will come out of a mediation.

Before a mediation with a potentially high conflict party, someone should determine whether the parties to the mediation are taking responsibility for their own behavior. One way is to interview employees who have been through coaching (such as the *New Ways for Work* coaching described in Chapter 13) to determine whether they are working on themselves in a meaningful way. "What is something that you are working on about yourself?" Or: "How would you deal with a similar situation in the future?"

The Power of Behavioral Agreements

Mediators should consider a process that focuses on behavioral agreements, about how to communicate verbally or in writing, make decisions, disagree, involve a higher-level supervisor if they reach an impasse, or even when to request third party support such as a union representative or a facilitator/mediator.

Mediation Skills That Can Transfer to the Workplace

The skills used in the *New Ways for Mediation* process are transferrable to the workplace: managed emotions, flexible thinking, making and responding to proposals, moderate behaviors, and checking ourselves. A workplace mediator can be a helpful source of information to the parties on behavioral agreements by telling them about agreements or protocols they have seen other people use successfully.

Michael remembers a mediation process in which an employee and a supervisor repeatedly triggered each other. The parties agreed to a behavioral protocol where one would raise their hand and calmly say "let's talk." This was to remind them both to try to speak as calmly as possible and try to focus on proposals versus complaints. In the mediation, they each used that signal at least 4-5 times. Ultimately, they carried it with them into the workplace effectively.

Another example is introducing the BIFF Response®, a method of responding to hostile or misinformed emails, texts, or other written communications in a manner that is Brief, Informative, Friendly, and Firm. Mediators can teach parties to use BIFF responses. HCPs are just as capable as anyone in learning this approach. They see hostility everywhere. Very often their toxic emails are, in their minds, a response to perceived attacks from others. BIFF responses are an excellent tool that the parties could agree in mediation to use with each other going forward. In the case of an HCP, we are unlikely to see perfection in the use of the BIFF Response approach, but remember that the goal is improvement, not to fix!

Using Proposals to Build Behavioral Agreements

In *New Ways for Mediation,* the mediator guides the parties to make and respond to proposals about behavioral agreements. This can involve a higher-level supervisor or manager to ensure agreements are monitored. The parties can also be prepared for this with skills-based coaching, as described in Chapters 12 and 13, and below.

Dealing with Breaches

A challenge that arises in workplace mediations is the question of who owns the agreement that the parties make. When there is a formal complaint pursuant to a harassment policy or collective agreement with a union, it is easy to see that a resolution in mediation will bring closure to the complaint, provided the correct internal procedures are followed. However, when a mediation occurs prior to a complaint being brought forward, it can be less clear who oversees the agreements that the parties might make with each other.

In our experience, what works well here is for the employer to have a policy stating that agreements made by employees in mediation should be written down and signed by the parties. This ensures that the agreements are more likely to be followed. Those recorded terms should be shared with the employer and should be considered binding upon the parties, so that the employer can hold them accountable for breaches. There should be an established protocol that the agreements made by the parties are owned by the employer and, therefore, failure to honor those agreements may result in consequences.

The same approach should apply with the obligation to keep the other contents of the discussions in mediation confidential. This should also be considered a duty to the employer as well as to each other. Many organizations have consequences for employees who breach a duty of confidentiality and we see a comparable duty to keep information from a mediation confidential. These terms should be included in any Agreement to Mediate.

Positive Advocates

We have found that mediations with HCPs can fall apart just hours, or even minutes after a joint session that seemed to go smoothly. With HCPs, this is not because an issue was not addressed, but because the HCP's perpetual state of discomfort gets triggered and they *still don't feel better*. They then escalate to thinking there must be something wrong with the agreement, or the mediator was biased against them. They then back track on the agreements that were made. To address this issue, mediators should be open to including positive third-party advocates in the mediation process. Third parties who are positive advocates for the HCP can be immensely helpful at all stages of the mediation process. These advocates may be a union/association representative, a friend, co-worker, or a coach. In preparing for mediation, these third parties can help the client practice new skills, remind them of the positive goals they wish to achieve, and the consequences of not reaching an agreement. They can also remind the HCP of information that was discussed in the initial meetings and help them craft proposals for the mediation. Skilled third parties can support the HCP in self-regulating their emotions when they get triggered into thinking about the past, inadvertently reminding themselves why they are so angry. In this way they can help the HCP focus on their own self-inter-est, problem-solving and the positive goals they wish to achieve.

In short, positive advocates can be valuable in mediation sessions by:

1. Helping the HCP stay emotionally regulated during joint ses-sions and when the mediator meets separately with the other party
2. Working with the HCP to make and respond to proposals
3. Reminding the HCP of the positive agreements they are mak-ing and shift them out of negativity and buyer's remorse

Preparation for Mediation (Coaching)

Preparing the parties for a mediation by teaching certain key skills is critical, while also assessing their ability to absorb the skills and suc-cessfully engage in the process.

Two different approaches to prepare people for mediation include:

1. The mediator provides pre-mediation coaching to each party, and
2. Separate coaches work with each party in advance.

The focus of the preparation is to work on four essential skills: *flexible thinking, managed emotions, moderate behavior* and *checking yourself.*

Coaching, Mediation, and Workplace Decision-Making

The following is a description of incorporating this coaching into me-diation and the overall workplace decision-making process.

First step: Workplace coaching (with an EAP, coach, or others)
The approach we recommend is to start with coaching. If possi-ble, start with coaching before any formal action or disciplinary action has been taken. This gives the opportunity to focus on the future, one of our strongest recommendations. As described in Chapter 13, we have developed the structured coaching method called *New Ways for Work: Personal Skills for Productive Relation-ships*, which is designed to teach basic conflict resolution tools that are increasingly lacking in today's blame-filled world.

This coaching method can be done in three sessions, either by an EAP, a coach who works for the organization or an outside therapist or coach. Each of these skills are included in the *New Ways for Work Workbook,* which includes several simple tools and practice exercises. The simplicity of this method and the positive emphasis on future problem-solving helps make it an appealing process. We have had many people say they appreciate these skills for their application to all areas of their lives.

By learning self-management skills in a coaching setting, many of the problem behaviors may be reduced or eliminated. There is no need for defensiveness with the coach, so employees or managers are more open to learning. Because it is short-term, employees don't feel unduly burdened or punished, which can block helpful learning. One or more parties to a dispute can learn these skills in their own coaching

Second Step: Determine if there is progress

After one or more parties to a dispute have gone through this coaching, someone can assess how seriously it has been taken. This could be a manager, human resources, or an outside consultant or mediator. Each individual can state what he or she is working on regarding their own self-management skills, such as: "I'm working on using more flexible thinking, so that I can see more solutions to problems that may come up." Or: "I'm working on managing my emotions better during a disagreement."

These types of statements indicate that progress can be made if the parties in conflict could sit down together. You don't want to have another bullying session. Instead, if those in the dispute can talk and listen to each other, while openly taking responsibility for managing their own behavior, then they may be able to move forward and resolve or reduce the workplace conflicts.

Of course, readiness for mediation should be determined after some coaching sessions have occurred. A common mistake occurs when asking two people in conflict to sit down and talk it out without learning any tools for doing that first. The emphasis has to be on learning skills, which can then be used to solve problems.

Third step: Mediation

Once it has been determined that a mediation is going to occur, the parties can be told to bring questions and proposals to the mediation. These are skills that they learn in *New Ways for Work* coaching to make the mediation more productive. When conflicts are particularly tense, this approach can help all parties stay focused on what to do in the future, based on their proposals. When people come in cold to a mediation, the risk of a blame game is high. So, we keep the focus on the future and on proposals and what to do going forward. This future-focused, proposal-focused approach has kept many conflicts from suddenly flaring up again. No one has to be defensive, because the future hasn't happened yet.

In addition, this preparation with coaching can help the parties be more successful in the mediation by minimizing or eliminating storytelling—talking about how awful the other person has been in the past, which tends to plunge the parties back into the dispute, causing tempers to easily flare. Instead, the need to do that will have been satisfied separately in coaching and the message that this will not be the focus will have been delivered.

Overall, it will be important to use a mediator who can keep this structure and discourage focusing on the past too much. Ideally, the mediator will be familiar with the skills taught in the *New Ways for Work* Coaching so that they can be reinforced and used to help resolve the issues in mediation.

Detailed Example: Family Issues Affecting the Workplace

The following is an example of how a mediation might proceed using the New Ways for Mediation method in a workplace situation. This example is drawn from the Workplace Mediation Role-Play #1: Family Issues in Appendix D. We will go through each of the stages in the New Ways for Mediation method.

Pre-Mediation with Alex, employee

The mediator decides to meet separately with each party for a confidential preparation session. As Alex is the complainant, the mediator decides to meet with Alex first. In this session, the mediator focuses on building rapport with Alex and then summarizes the mediation process and answers questions. The mediator then coaches Alex with the Client Pre-Mediation Handout (Appendix B) and gives Alex a copy of the handout to hold onto. The mediator works through each skill, reviewing the document with Alex and working with Alex to think through how Alex will use each skill. The mediator helps Alex think of an encouraging statement Alex can use in the mediation. Alex chooses, "I am a good employee, I can get through this!" Alex writes this down and repeats it silently several times. The mediator encourages Alex to remember the phrase and use it when feeling anxious before or during the mediation.

The mediator then moves to flexible thinking and here reviews how it is important to think of proposals Alex wants to make about important issues. The mediator explains this could be two alternatives (A or B) that are offered to the supervisor to choose from, or one is offered with the other proposal as backup (A then a B). This will help both Alex and Robin think flexibly about how to solve the problems. The mediator coaches Alex to think of two proposals for each issue, to help Alex get comfortable with the approach and tasks Alex to think of proposals for any other issues as homework.

If Alex were to get stuck on creating a proposal, the mediator could offer three options for Alex to think about but always finish with "but it's up to you." Alex thinks of two proposals for what to do if Alex must leave work on short notice to deal with their daughter. Alex decides to propose A – Alex briefs the supervisor on any key issues before leaving, or B – Alex maintains a running log of key tasks and their status; that way if Alex has to leave on short notice, the supervisor knows what is happening.

Finally, the mediator walks Alex through the skill of moderate behaviors and gives concrete examples and then asks Alex if there is one of the skills Alex wants to practice. Alex decides to practice "I" language. The mediator asks if there is anything the supervisor might say in the mediation that would cause Alex to react negatively that Alex could practice. Alex thinks the supervisor might say, "You are behind on all your work—you have to do better!" The mediator works with Alex to come up with a phrase to say back, in this case "I need you to tell me which tasks are the priorities. I can then focus on those."

The mediator and Alex then role-play the conversation to allow Alex to get comfortable using "I" language. First, the mediator plays Alex and Alex plays the supervisor. Alex says to the mediator "Alex, you are behind on your work, you need to catch up!" The mediator replies with Alex's chosen phrase and then asks Alex how that landed. Alex decides the phrase seemed to work. The mediator and Alex swap roles and the mediator plays the supervisor and Alex practices responding with "I" language. Alex is starting to feel a bit more confident about the mediation. The mediator asks if Alex has any other questions and the preparation session ends.

Pre-Mediation with Robin, supervisor

The mediator takes a similar approach with Robin. In this case, the focus of the discussion ends up being how Robin gets stressed when Alex gets escalated and either wants to avoid the situation and end the meeting or gets flustered and blurts out something unhelpful. The mediator coaches Robin to also use "I" language to focus on Alex's behavior such as "Your voice is very loud, and I can't concentrate on what I am saying. This is an important conversation for both of us, but I need to do it where we are both using a conversational tone, or we can take a break." Robin is feeling more confident about the mediation and tells the mediator Robin can see using these skills in the workplace.

The mediator follows the 4 Stages of the New Ways for Mediation method. Let's look at issues in each stage:

Stage 1: Establishing the Process

In Stage 1, Alex interrupts the mediator to say "I can only stay for one session and if everything isn't finished, I have to carry on with a formal complaint. My union rep says this probably isn't going to work anyway." (This wasn't true. The union rep had encouraged Alex that resolving issues through mediation was a good approach and that Alex was at risk of losing this job.) Robin gets upset and says, "That's not fair, I thought we had agreed to three sessions." The mediator responds, "We will be talking about whether to book additional sessions shortly. First, I must explain the process to you, so you'll know what to expect and what your part is. This will be very brief. It is what I've found to be the most helpful to do. So, I appreciate your patience. Thanks." Then the mediator calmly keeps walking the process forward, and in this way establishes the mediator's authority for managing the process, allowing people to get comfortable with the process before making big decisions.

Stage 2: Making their Agenda
They easily agreed on the big topics for discussion.

Stage 3: Making Proposals
The parties make and respond to proposals on what to do if Alex requests to leave work on short notice due to a situation with their daughter. Alex has the two proposals ready (Alex prepared these in pre-mediation coaching), and first proposes to brief the supervisor before leaving. The supervisor starts to respond by saying, "That's not going to work because you will interrupt me doing something important." Alex starts to get upset, saying to the mediator, "See, Robin isn't interested in any of my ideas!"

The mediator calmly says "This is an important issue for both of you. Alex, you want to be able to leave quickly to attend to your daughter, and you also want to make sure Robin is up-to-speed on the situation. Robin, you want to make sure you can focus on your own priorities and so can't always stop to talk to Alex if Alex needs to leave." Both Alex and Robin agree with the mediator's reflection of their needs (interests).

The mediator then redirects them back into the proposals task and says to Robin, "It sounds like your answer to Alex's proposal is a "No." Do you have a proposal you would like to make back, that might address the needs you both have?" Robin decides to propose that Alex send Robin an email saying Alex has to leave, and that as long as Alex can maintain a log of where all files are at, and keeps it up to date, they can arrange a meeting the next day to deal with anything that is left over. Alex agrees to the proposal. The mediator summarizes the agreement on the whiteboard, and they move onto the next issue.

Stage 4: Making their Decisions
Alex and Robin work out several more agreements and the mediator prepares a written memorandum summarizing them. In the document, they agree to use certain communication protocols including the Proposals skill for important issues they need to agree upon and BIFF Responses when responding to each other by email. They also request the manager authorize New Ways for Work coaching for each of them. Alex and Rob-

in sign the document and it is shared with the manager. The employer has a policy that written agreements coming out of a mediation process are binding on the parties.

Conclusion

Successful mediation of workplace issues is very important because employees, managers, and colleagues are required to spend so much time together. There are many issues to consider, including suitability for mediation, managing expectations, creating behavioral agreements, and pre-mediation coaching—such as with the New Ways for Work Coaching method which emphasizes the same four skills as the *New Ways for Mediation* method: managed emotions, flexible thinking, moderate behavior, and checking yourself. All put together, these tips and methods can bring greater peace to the workplace and help employees, managers, and colleagues thrive together and enjoy their work.

CHAPTER 15

Divorce Mediation Issues

Most divorce mediation issues have been addressed throughout the prior chapters. However, here are some further considerations:

- Additional issues for each stage
- High conflict versus domestic violence
- Domestic violence concerns
- Videoconferencing: joint or shuttle

Additional Issues for Each Stage

Stage 1: Establishing the Process. When explaining the process, emphasize that there is room in most states for being creative in developing the terms of a divorce agreement or parenting plan for unmarried couples. Encourage them to make it work for them.

On the other hand, the mediator should also say that divorce and parenting plans are legal decisions which can have a lot of requirements or standards that the parties need to know. If they do not have lawyers, the mediator should encourage them to at least consult with lawyers before making their decisions.

However, you should also point out to the parties that their decisions are up to them (with a few legal restraints) and they should evaluate what they are told rather than allowing lawyers to drive their case. There are many helpful, mediation-friendly lawyers in most communities; however, there are also some who will persuade a party to drop out of mediation and go to court when it is not in their best interest to do so. Get a second opinion if you are unsure what to do.

Stage 2: Making their Agenda. When asking for their *Thoughts* *and Questions* about the decisions they are facing, it helps to have them specifically address five key areas: parenting plan, child support, spousal support (alimony), property and debt division, and any timing concerns (anyone moving, impending court dates, etc.). You can then give them general information (not legal advice or direction) that they might not have thought about. This helps to get them in the same ballpark in terms of general expectations, may make their expectations more realistic, and helps them think about possible proposals they will make.

It's much better to get this information out before they make their proposals, so they don't feel betrayed by you if one makes a proposal that is usually prohibited (such as proposing to permanently terminate child support while a child is still a minor, when the door always has to be left open for the court to address the issue).

Stage 3: Making their Proposals. Proposals about parenting plans can be one of the most difficult areas in divorce mediation. High conflict parents often have widely differing viewpoints. "I should be the primary parent and you can see them on alternate weekends." "No, I should have 50-50 parenting time." This is a common starting dilemma for parents. It often helps to say: "This is a common starting dilemma, yet most parents find an agreement somewhere in between these two possibilities." Don't be rattled by their seeming impasse right from the start. Create an expectation for negotiating something that eventually fits for them. Let them know that the vast majority of parents eventually resolve these dilemmas.

One approach is to help them develop a very short-term parenting plan, which they can try and then revise based on experience. Sometimes just figuring out a two-week plan or a one-month plan can work, which can be reviewed at the next mediation session. Experience is a great teacher and this often helps them become more realistic and slightly more flexible.

If you only have very limited time with the parties for making parenting agreements, such as in a community or court-based mediation program, you can send out an instruction sheet to the parties stating that they should come to the mediation prepared with items for their agenda and 1-2 proposals for each issue they want to raise. With such preparation, we have heard of programs that have been able to go quickly into negotiating parenting plans and have helped the parties reach agreements in just one hour.

Stage 4: Making their Decisions. High conflict couples often have the finalization of their divorce agreements take almost as long as the decision-making process. It can take weeks or months sometimes to get the wording just right to satisfy both parties (and their lawyers, if any). It helps to be matter of fact about that, so that it doesn't escalate unnecessarily. Warn them about this when it is time to start writing up the final divorce agreement. They can always make new agreements until it is signed. Then it can become much more complicated to change things in many cases, such as final property division that has already been distributed.

Warn them about buyer's remorse, to encourage them to develop enough details of their agreements so that things won't unravel after they are done. For example, you can say:

"In some cases—probably not yours—the parties don't always follow through on what they have agreed upon. So, it's best to think of everything beforehand in order to ensure that the terms of the agreement are complete and enforceable enough to be followed. You can put in terms about what to do if either of you don't fulfill any parts of the agreement, such as small fines, changes in the parenting plan, or other consequences. It's best to think of them now."

Some high conflict people rarely do what they promised to do. For example, reimbursing the other party for joint expenses, making payments for getting the house, and caring for the child during their scheduled parenting time. It helps to think up consequences for each of these possibilities. For example, it's a good idea to get a lien on a house to secure monthly payments or a lump sum payment later on. Some couples require an annual exchange of copies of their income tax returns to confirm any income changes over the course of the year. (Of course, some high conflict people lie to the Internal Revenue Service as much as they lie to their spouses.)

High Conflict versus Domestic Violence

Historically, there has been an ongoing debate about high conflict families versus families with domestic violence. They are frequently considered to be very different types of families. Some have viewed high conflict families as involving two equally difficult and aggressive parties who simply can't get along and can't stop fighting. It is common for judges, lawyers, and others to tell such families that they just need to "get over it." On the other hand, families with domestic violence have an individual perpetrator who needs to be restrained and the rest of the family protected from that person.

In reality, based on our experiences over decades of family law cases, in and out of court, this is an unhelpful comparison. We think in terms of high conflict personalities *with domestic violence* and high conflict personalities *without domestic violence*. There are many so-called *high conflict families* who have one individual with a high conflict personality and the other party is a reasonable person. In fact, from our surveys, about half of high conflict cases have only one high conflict personality.

Therefore, it will help all family law professionals, including mediators, to realize that not all families have individuals who are equally contributing to the problems in the family. In fact, the term *high conflict family* should no longer be used. It is important to realize that many are actually families in which there is domestic violence or an individual who is engaged in other extreme behavior that must be stopped. This possibility must be taken seriously. Remember the three theories of the high conflict case mentioned in Chapter 4: Preparing Yourself.

Domestic Violence Concerns

We have already addressed screening for domestic violence in Pre-Mediation Coaching. However, screening must be an ongoing issue. Survivors may lie about having no history of domestic violence or they may not understand that they have been a victim of domestic violence. Then conversations or issues may arise where the mediator starts to wonder if violence is a possibility.

For example, the husband in one young couple was surprisingly rigid and demanding about a 50-50 parenting plan for their one-year-old child. He had not been providing much of the care before the separation, so that the mother thought a much more gradual increase in parenting time was appropriate. Financial issues were difficult as well, primarily because of the husband's rigidity and demanding approach to the negotiations. However, prior to the mediation the wife had expressed no history or concerns about domestic violence.

The morning after the first mediation session, the wife called the mediation office and told the paralegal office manager that the husband had confronted her aggressively by her car in the parking garage after they left the session. He told the wife that he was so frustrated with her that he "felt like hurting her." He didn't touch her and drove away. The wife told the paralegal that she really wanted to complete the whole divorce in mediation, but she also felt concerned about his difficulty negotiating without getting frustrated and irritable. She didn't want the mediator to tell the husband that she had called.

The mediator decided to have the paralegal tell both parties that he had been thinking about their case and that their issues were so complicated that he would not meet with them again unless they both had lawyers in the mediation room with them to help resolve these complicated issues. This way the mediator didn't need to speak to either of the parties about the wife's call and didn't need to say why he made this requirement. They both came to the next session with lawyers and the case proceeded as a fairly normal case, with the husband much more relaxed and his lawyer helping him understand the law and focusing on making productive proposals.

This result helped the mediator preserve his policy of not communicating with the parties between sessions and remaining impartial, while also ensuring a safe process by setting limits on the structure of the mediation process by requiring the presence of lawyers.

But concerns about safety and voluntariness of agreements in possible domestic violence cases go beyond the actual mediation sessions themselves. Threats and fears can be triggered simply by the discussions and agreements which extend well after the mediation. So, the nature and possible imbalance of the agreements that come out of the mediation should also be considered.

With all of this in mind, the question of whether the parties should see each other in a videoconference mediation should also be considered. This is addressed with some research below under videoconferencing.

Videoconferencing: Joint or Shuttle

With the Covid-19 pandemic of 2020 and beyond, the use of videoconferencing became widespread with divorce and parenting mediations out of necessity. But it also became quite popular because of its convenience. One of its seeming benefits in domestic violence cases is that a survivor of domestic violence can be totally safe, appearing from an unknown location. However, this raises the question of whether the parties should see each other on the video screen. While at first it seems like this should not be a problem because there is no danger on a video screen, it can still trigger feelings of fear and manipulations by an aggressor.

A study before COVID was done, then published in 2021, compared litigation to in-person shuttle mediation and videoconference mediation. This was mentioned in Chapter 12: Pre-Mediation Coaching under Screening. Here is more information, quoting an excerpt from the abstract for that study:

> *Both mediation approaches [shuttle in office versus joint videoconferencing] were perceived as safe by mediators, and parents felt safer in mediation than in traditional litigation. Parents in mediation were also more satisfied with the process than parents in traditional litigation. Return-to-court cases took 3 times as long to reach final resolution as mediation cases. Mediators tended to prefer shuttle over videoconferencing, and videoconferencing cases were half as likely to reach agreement as cases in shuttle. Through coding the content of the document*

that resolved case issues, we found no statistically significant group differences in legal custody, physical custody, or parenting time arrangements, and few differences in the likelihood of the document specifying a variety of arrangements (e.g., how to handle missed parenting time) or including safety provisions (e.g., supervised child exchanges).[18]

One could interpret the preference for and success of shuttle mediation to the fact that the parties were not distracted or triggered by seeing each other's faces and hearing each other's voices. Since the study was done and all mediations went to videoconferencing in 2020 with COVID, this would suggest that it would be better for a mediator who is using videoconferencing to use the breakout rooms, going back-and-forth with each party, rather than having them together on the screen. One of the authors of this study has agreed with this possibility.

This further suggests that those with high conflict personalities without violence, but who are constantly triggering one or both party's defensiveness, might also benefit from shuttle mediation with breakout rooms when using videoconferencing. This is a suggestion to discuss with each party during a pre-mediation coaching session if videoconferencing is being considered.

Detailed Example:
Divorce Mediation Demonstration on Website

A 3-hour recorded video demonstration of a divorce mediation with Bill Eddy is available on the High Conflict Institute website, www. HighConflictInstitute.com, under training. A PDF handout of the explanatory PowerPoint slides are contained in this book in Appendix C: Mediation Demonstration PowerPoint Slides. At the end of the slides are slides listing the Table of Contents; Index: Explaining Key Issues; and Index: Managing Controversies.

Conclusion

This chapter has addressed the value of several additional strategies that can be considered in doing divorce and parenting mediation in high conflict cases. In addition, the importance of ongoing screening of the potential for domestic violence has grown as some high conflict people become increasingly aggressive in today's relationships. It's important to know that there are high conflict people with violence and high conflict people without violence, and that the difference is often not obvious on the surface. For this reason, the term *high conflict family* should be discontinued and the possibility of one high conflict person must be considered. (Remember the 3 theories of any high conflict case in Chapter 4.)

Given the increased use of videoconferencing since 2020, a mediator and the parties should consider whether to use shuttle mediation with breakout rooms instead of joint appearances on the video screen. This could apply when known domestic violence cases are being mediated, but also could be used when high conflict individuals without domestic violence are involved. Their emotions and behavior may prove too distracting and over-stimulating, whether it's a case of one high conflict person or two.

CHAPTER 16

Group (Such as Elder Mediation) Issues

Group mediations involve several people, any one of whom or more might have high conflict personalities. One type of group mediation that is occurring more frequently these days is elder mediation and estate mediation. This chapter will use elder mediation as an example for any group mediation.

This chapter is to be distinguished from the next chapter on Large Group Facilitation, as this chapter addresses situations in which a group needs to make decisions to resolve a conflict that it shares. In the Large Group Facilitation chapter, we are addressing meetings with potential strangers who have no prior relationship and no specific conflicts with each other, but still may need to manage one or more HCPs who show up.

We will address additional issues by the stages of our method:

Setting Up the Mediation: One of the first issues will be whether to have shuttle or joint mediation sessions. Many elder and estate mediators prefer to meet separately with everyone to avoid high emotions and high conflict behavior. There is certainly something to say for that. However, we believe that when people have ongoing relationships—such as in families—that it is preferable to meet jointly even if there are one or two high conflict people expected.

This is a question of the mediator's comfort level with the level of likely conflict. Using the structure and tools of *New Ways for Mediation,* a mediator may feel confident that he or she can manage a family involved in the decisions at hand. If it does not go well, then the mediator can switch to shuttle mediation and meet separately in caucus with each party or small groups who get along. In planning, it would be important to have breakout rooms available for in-person mediations, or knowledge of operating breakout rooms in virtual mediations.

Pre-Mediation Coaching: It is important to engage in individual meetings prior to a full joint mediation session when there are several people involved, such as adult children, spouse, and other siblings of an elder who needs care. The Pre-Mediation Coaching process described in Chapter 12 can be easily used for this purpose.

One addition to the process described in Chapter 12 would be asking each person about the group dynamics and suggestions for what roles people will likely take, such as a leader, an ally, a disrupter, and so forth. Find out who is a source of various types of information. Sometimes one party has been caring for the elder and will have inside information but may also have deeper frustrations or appear to be manipulating or abusing the elder.

There are often unresolved sibling issues that can come to a head when making elder care decisions. For example, one sibling may have been favored ("Mother always liked you best!") or one sibling may have been uninvolved in the family for decades while the other has been a primary caregiver. There is sometimes a family friend who has become a key person who should not be left out. There may be another family member who does not want that family friend involved.

All of these issues can be identified by the mediator during Pre-Mediation Coaching. Yet it will be essential for the mediator to teach them all that the mediator must be seen as in charge of the process; otherwise, the mediator will likely be over-run in any joint sessions. With several people involved, the chances of one or more HCPs are much more likely these days. Building individual relationships and realistic expectations of the process will be essential.

Stage 1: Establishing the Process. If you do joint sessions, it will be very important to show that you are in charge of the process. It is recommended that you stand at least at the start, to physically establish your authority, if possible, while everyone else is sitting. Certainly, it will be essential that the group is quiet while you are speaking, so that you temporarily stop diversionary issues from taking over, as described in Chapter 7: Stage 1: Establishing the Process.

Stage 2: Making their Agenda. Depending on what you have found out during your Pre-Mediation Coaching sessions, you may decide to solicit agenda items before a group meeting, or you may decide to build the agenda at the beginning of each joint meeting. Remember, by making the parties responsible for making the agenda, you get them busy thinking rather than reacting to each other.

It is often helpful to build the agenda as a group, using a white board or flip chart, in person or virtually. This gives the group a team project with relatively easy joint decision-making to start off with and build momentum. Which topics are important? What order should they be addressed? You want to take the approach of *building a team against the problems*, rather than allowing people to define the conflict as me against you. It may help to simply go around the room in order of how they are seated, with the mediator picking where to start, so that the HCP is treated as simply one of the members of the group, rather than giving them excessive time if they try to dominate a discussion.

You can establish boundaries by giving each person a turn—a short turn—to speak in building the agenda. This way, if an HCP interrupts, you can emphasize that they will have a turn when it gets to them very soon. That way you're not just shutting them off, but rather re-directing them. Then, when it's their turn to contribute with proposed agenda items, you can limit their time just like you have limited the others who went before, since HCPs often have a hard time stopping themselves.

Stage 3: Making their Proposals. With a group, it often helps to have people prepare written proposals beforehand, so that they are ready to be discussed and analyzed. The mediator can use the same 3-step process described in Chapter 9: Making their Proposals, but it may take much longer with questions and it may help to write the questions on the white board or flip chart—again, to reinforce the theme of building a team against the problems.

Stage 4: Making their Decisions. This may be much more complex if there are legal decisions, care-giving decisions, or moving into a residential facility decisions. But the process of step-by-step analyzing proposals and coming to decisions can be used. Getting the details figured out will be essential and the mediator will want to keep track of who is doing what task. The mediator should also know what issues need to be addressed that the parties may not have thought of.

Detailed Example: The Contested Family Home

The following example is drawn from several of our experiences with elder mediations. This could be quite a complex scenario, so we have deliberately simplified it to focus on the process versus the legal issues that might be involved. In this situation there are four adult siblings who are caught up in a disagreement that has escalated to the point of lawyers being hired. A court case is close to being filed.

The mother, Alice, is 85 years old and is in a senior's care home and is not competent to give legal instructions. The youngest son, Robert, is living in the family home and says he is maintaining it for Alice until she returns, and that she said she wanted him to live in it and manage it while she was not able. He is the successor trustee on her trust and all four children are beneficiaries when she dies.

The three eldest siblings want the family home to be sold to fund Alice's care and eliminate the expenses of maintaining the house. They see Robert as a "squatter" and that he is taking advantage of the situation, as Alice is clearly never going to return home. There are no written instructions from Alice on what to do with the family home. The best outcome is that the children agree on what to do. Robert has retained a lawyer and the other three siblings have retained a lawyer. They agree to attend mediation before filing a court action.

The mediator knows the most likely reason why the mediation will fail is not because the legal issues are too complicated, but because one or all of the party's emotions will get in the way of their resolution. Further, the mediator sees from the history that there is high conflict behavior on both sides. In this case, the mediator decides to use the New Ways for Mediation method as it focuses on the future, versus the past, and stays away from opening up emotions (which in this situation, the parties would likely drown in).

Pre-Mediation Coaching
The mediator starts by first meeting individually with each sibling. The mediator explains the mediation process and coaches each party with the

Client Pre-Mediation Handout on the skills to use during the mediation.

Stage 1: Establishing the Process

At the joint session, Robert and the siblings each bring a lawyer. One of the siblings brings their partner as a support person, another attends by live videoconference. In this case the mediator is careful to meet with the lawyers together before starting the full group mediation, to provide them with information about the New Ways for Mediation process and to encourage the lawyers to help their clients prepare at least two proposals for each important issue and then enlist them in managing the emotional climate in the room. The lawyers are cooperative and want to help the parties resolve this without lots of acrimony.

Stage 2: Making their Agenda

The mediator knows that establishing and maintaining control over the process will be key, so the mediator decides to implement the use of a talking piece (which the mediator can give out or take back) to make it clear who has the floor. The mediator introduces guidelines for the talking piece, including that only the person with the talking piece can speak (except the mediator). The mediator goes around the room and gives each person an opportunity to propose Agenda items. Robert is belligerent, but the mediator matter-of-factly emphasizes that he gets his turn and writes down his proposed Agenda items, then proceeds to the next person. An Agenda is agreed upon, including future communication among the siblings.

Stage 3: Making their Proposals

Supporting the parties to make and respond to proposals with a group can be more complex but with some planning it can be highly effective. During the session, the lawyers prove very helpful de-escalating their clients' emotions, keeping them focused on the future and redirecting their clients to focus on making proposals, asking questions, and responding to proposals. The mediator reflected back what the mediator saw as important in the siblings' proposals.

Despite everyone's best efforts, it seemed like they would still reach an impasse as Robert was still proposing that he be allowed to live in the house indefinitely and the other siblings were proposing that he move out immediately. One of the lawyers noticed that Robert seemed quite concerned about his finances as he had only recently started working again. The lawyer asked to meet with the mediator and the other lawyer. The lawyers suggested that if the mediator proposed an option that found some middle ground, everyone might be able to find resolution. The mediator advised that in the mediator's experience, proposing only one solution could easily result in more impasse. (See Chapter 9, under Educating about 3 Options) Instead, they agreed that the mediator would suggest three scenarios to stimulate more discussion:

1. *Robert be given 6 months to obtain financing to purchase the house*
2. *Robert could live in the house for some agreed-upon number of months, and then the house would be sold and the proceeds put into an account to pay for Alice's care*
3. *The mediation would end now and the parties proceed to court to have a judge decide*

Stage 4: Making their Decisions
The mediator met privately with Robert and his lawyer, then with the three older siblings and their lawyer to discuss the options. They eventually agreed to the second scenario, giving Robert 6 more months of residence and then Robert would sell the house and put the proceeds into an account for Alice's care.

Conclusion

In any group mediation, the same basic procedure of the *New Ways for Mediation* method can be used. In this chapter we focused on elder and estate issues, which increasingly involve high conflict family members. By meeting with each of the family members individually, the mediator was able to get an idea of what to expect. Since it was a family matter, the mediator decided to proceed with joint sessions. The focus was on their proposals, but they got stuck. The mediator then offered three scenarios of possible outcomes to help them get their thinking un-stuck. By using three scenarios, it isn't like the mediator is making the decision for them, but rather giving them some tips they could use and adapt for themselves. Finally, the mediator ended up meeting with the parties in separate caucuses.

This is one option that can be used more or less, as the mediator believes appropriate. This type of dispute is particularly suited for the *New Ways for Mediation* approach, so that the parties can work together and get credit for their resolution.

CHAPTER 17

Large Group Facilitation

High conflict people are showing up in more and more large group and public meetings these days. Homeowners Associations hold regular public meetings for their members. Businesses hold meetings of stakeholders in their development projects, such as new construction or utility planning. Schools and communities have public meetings. Any organization or committee may hold large group meetings for any purpose. This issue is especially important in volunteer organizations, church groups, nonprofits and other groups, because everyone else is trying to be nice and may not be used to managing a high conflict person.

This chapter is different from the prior chapter on group mediation, because this focuses on meetings in which there may be no issue requiring mediation, but in which a high conflict person can cause serious disruption and distress. The following approach can be used in groups as large as hundreds or as few as a handful of people.

A Respectful Meeting Policy

Disrespectful meeting behavior can include constantly interrupting the meeting chairperson or other participants, opposing the pre-planned agenda, inviting inappropriate people to the meeting, coming late and disrupting the progress of the meeting, taking calls in front of others, unnecessarily surfing the Internet, disparaging remarks or disregard for women, younger employees, older employees, different racial or ethnic groups, yelling, dramatically walking out, throwing paper, and so forth.

It is especially difficult when the disruptive person(s) has information the group needs but is behaving in this manner. Some people are oblivious to their impact on the group discussion, while others enjoy the power. They have to be disruptive because they have important information and see themselves as superior to the group.

Regardless of the motivations, here are five suggestions:

1. Post a Policy

Whether a policy is posted on the wall of a meeting room, or on small cards on a table, it can help set the tone for a meeting, especially if there are outsiders who don't know how meetings are run at a particular office. It shows the organization's support for respectful meetings from the top on down. This can be similar to No Smoking signs or other common warnings. The policy could say something like this:

> *Respectful Meeting Policy*
>
> *At _____ organization, much of our work is accomplished at meetings. In order to ensure the smooth, respectful, and efficient management of meetings, the meeting chair shall manage the Agenda and the right of members to speak. On rare occasion, a meeting member may become disrespectful in communicating their information and opinions. In such a case, the meeting chair shall ask the meeting member to revise their manner of speech to be respectful. In the event that the meeting member does not thereafter speak respectfully, the chair may announce a short break or end the meeting, in the meeting chair's discretion. Other meeting members shall support the chair in making such decisions.[19]*

With such a policy announcement somewhere, a meeting chairperson can refer to it in the event that someone becomes disruptive or disrespectful. It will also strengthen the other group members to support the chairperson in enforcing this policy. Furthermore, it shows that the organization values the input of everyone and will not tolerate individuals who attempt to hijack the agenda or the running of a meeting.

2. Immediate Intervention by Meeting Chair

When such disruptions or disparaging remarks occur, many meeting chairs are caught off-guard, and they stop and just listen to the disruptive person while trying to figure out what to do. It can be quite jarring when someone suddenly goes in the opposite direction of the meeting. In such cases, the meeting chair is encouraged to immediately assert their role as chair of the meeting and interrupt the disruptive person. They can say something like:

> *"We appreciate your interest in expressing your point of view. However, this is not the right time [or right manner] for you to do so. Please hold off for now [or speak in a calmer tone], so that we can stay focused on our Agenda. Now, we were discussing..."*

Then the meeting chair should change eye contact to the others in the room. By quickly doing this, the disruptive person does not gain traction or attention for being disruptive. This is especially important in volunteer organizations, nonprofits and other groups where everyone else is trying to be nice. Unfortunately, when dealing with a high conflict person, you have to be immediate and assertive, otherwise they will hijack the meeting.

3. Other Participants Support the Meeting Chairperson

One of the common characteristics of high-conflict people is that they are always recruiting negative advocates. It is not unusual that a meeting disrupter turns to other meeting members for support in challenging the agenda and taking over the meeting. Or making a disparaging remark and then turning to other meeting members to try to get a laugh out of them. Generally, when meeting participants realize this dynamic, they should just avoid paying attention to the disrupter, so that the meeting chair can maintain control of the meeting.

Another way that participants can be helpful is to gently admonish the person making disparaging remarks or being otherwise disruptive, but saying something like: "That's enough, Joe." And then immediately turning their attention back to the meeting chair. It isn't necessary to stop everything to give a long speech about how inappropriate someone else is being. This can be done very quickly, with a minimum of effort.

In some cases, the whole group can just stay focused on the meeting chair and not give the disruptive person any attention at all. Since the goal of most high conflict people is to get attention, this will either slow them down or they will leave.

4. Establish the Agenda in Advance

One of the easiest ways to get group support for the meeting is to give people an opportunity to contribute to the Agenda in advance of the meeting. Then, the final meeting Agenda can be posted or distributed before the meeting occurs.

Then, it is very difficult for a meeting disrupter to hijack the Agenda. Often, they want to throw out the Agenda and replace it with their seemingly much more urgent issue. Or they sometimes say that the presumptions underlying today's Agenda are all wrong, so we have to go back to start. They say: "It's pointless to proceed until we have this larger discussion." (Such as the group's goals.) While that might be a good idea at some point, it doesn't mean that anyone gets to hijack today's meeting and the Agenda that has already been prepared.

If they attempt to do that, the meeting chairperson can simply say: "We all agreed on this Agenda in advance, so please stop raising this new issue now. You'll have to save it for another day."

5. Disinvite the Meeting Disrupter to Future Meetings

When there is a continual meeting disrupter or disrespectful person, it may be necessary to disinvite them to future meetings, so that the group can get on with the business at hand. In some cases, if the person has necessary knowledge or information, they may attend by video or phone. Ironically, when this has been done, high conflict people still engage in their disruptive behavior—although it is less disruptive and can be turned off. This is an example of how stuck some high conflict people can be.

Detailed Example: Derek the Disruptor

Derek has decided to join a planning committee for a volunteer group that is planning an annual conference and fundraiser. The committee meetings are open to any member of the group. He arrives late for the meeting, momentarily distracting everyone as he is carrying a stack of papers that he is barely able to hold under his arm. People make room for him to sit at the long table with a dozen other people attending.

Carrie is running the meeting. "As I was saying, the next item on the Agenda is to decide who is going to be in charge of publicity for the annual event. Who of you would like to volunteer for this subcommittee?"

Three people raise their hands, including Derek.

Derek says: "Before we go any further, I think that we need to discuss the budget for this committee. I mean, how do we know what we can do without knowing the budget?"

Carrie says: "That is going to be one of the first tasks of the committee: figuring out what the various forms of publicity cost so that we can consider several choices at our next meeting. Right, Bonnie?"

Bonnie: "That's right. As chair of the subcommittee, I will be raising that at our meetings."

Derek: "But wait a minute! That's backwards. We need to simply decide on a budget, so that the subcommittee knows what it has to work with. Can't you see that?"

Carrie: "Derek, that's already been decided. We decided that before you arrived. Now, let's go to our next topic on the Agenda."

Derek: "But that's ridiculous. Carrie, you obviously are too young to know how budgets need to be developed first." Derek turns to Sam, the other person who raised his hand to be on the Publicity subcommittee. "Sam, you look like a successful businessman. Tell them how important it is to develop the budget first."

Sam: "Well, uh, there's different ways that you can do it. Some groups do it first, and some check out the current costs of various forms of publicity and then decide on their budget."

Carrie quickly interrupts: "Actually, guys. Let's hold on right there. We need to stay focused on the Agenda and this topic has already been decided. I would appreciate it if everyone stays focused and does not get drawn into any cross-talk. Derek, you need to follow the meeting Agenda and respect my role as the meeting chair. Otherwise, I will need to halt the meeting and have us take a break. Can you agree to let me continue with the planned Agenda?"

Derek: "Sure, fine. Whatever you say." And he leans back in his chair and the meeting proceeds without further disruption.

In this case, Carrie was swift in setting limits on Derek. Fortunately, her assertive and firm interruption of his crosstalk was accepted by Derek and Sam. However, in some cases, there needs to be a pre-meeting planning session with other committee or board members, so that they can be reminded not to engage in any crosstalk with a disruptive person. They also need to agree to follow the meeting chair in standing up and taking a break if necessary. If it is a meeting on a virtual platform or a large group meeting with a microphone for open comments, there can be an agreed-upon plan that the meeting chair can turn off the microphone of a disruptive person.

Conclusion

Hopefully, most people have not faced this problem yet. However, it does appear to be increasing and you will be better off to be prepared—rather than caught by surprise—by having suggestions such as these readily available. It also helps to practice intervening like Carrie did before a large group meeting (this same example is in Appendix D as a role-play), so that you can be comfortable with setting limits and are used to saying the words you want to use in front of others.

CHAPTER 18

Ethical Issues

High conflict people seem to be the ones most likely to sue their professionals, employers, friends, and family members. Mediators are rarely sued, but it does happen. It helps to be careful when dealing with high conflict people. The following are a dozen tips to keep in mind to avoid getting sued or involved in an administrative action or public complaint.

1. Avoid creating unrealistic expectations.
HCPs tend toward all-or-nothing thinking, which means that they can have extremely positive expectations as well as extremely negative ones. Be careful not to over-sell the ability of the mediation process to resolve all disputes and be careful not to over-sell yourself in order to get business. Be matter of fact in explaining what you can and cannot do. Remind yourself that you do not need to take this case. There will be plenty more.

2. Avoid trying to shift power and attention to or from an HCP.
Treat both parties as equal in the mediation process. If you find that you like one party better than the other, make sure that this does not show. Do not try to take power away from an HCP. If one is acting like a bully, shift to meeting separately with each party in caucus or make it clear that you are not invested in them reaching an agreement. Tell them to get outside legal advice. Likewise, do not focus all of your empathy, attention and respect statements on just one party.

3. Avoid directing anger at your client(s).
You will be frustrated. You will be irritated. Prepare for this by reminding yourself "It's not about me" and "I'm not responsible for their outcome." (See other encouraging statements in Chapter 4 under Putting On Your Armor.) This will help you keep your cool even when they

are acting badly. If you confront them with anger—no matter how justified—they will escalate the confrontation much higher than you can imagine. You will become their next target of blame.

4. Avoid working harder than your client(s).
High conflict people frequently try to put all the responsibility on their professionals and friends for resolving their disputes. It is important to keep the responsibility for their behavior, decisions, and conflicts on their own shoulders. Your job is to *assist them,* using the appropriate standard of care for your profession and community. If they pressure you to fix something, you can gently say: "You folks have a dilemma. Let's look at some of your options for resolving it."

5. Avoid directing your clients to make certain agreements.
Mediators run the risk of the unauthorized practice of law (UPL) if they give their clients advice or direction toward certain outcomes. Even when lawyers practice mediation, it is important that they avoid giving advice or direction when they are a neutral mediator. This is extra important when high conflict people are involved because they will blame you for any outcome but their own (and they might blame you for that too). Keep decisions on their shoulders.

6. Avoid working without the ongoing agreement of your clients.
It is safest to have your clients consent to each step of the mediation process, including whether to proceed on a topic or change topics. ("I suggest that we move on to the next topic now, is that okay with you two?") Sending follow-up letters or summaries may help to clarify what they have said and what you have said, so that there are no misunderstandings. This also avoids parties saying that you made them do something or would not let them do something.

7. Avoid bending your own rules.
It's easy to absorb the anxiety of HCPs and feel tempted to do something extra to help them calm down. Don't! Firm boundaries, clear expectations, and clear roles are necessary when working with high conflict clients. That's the only way you can truly help them. If you try to rescue them from themselves or clean up their messes, you will get punished for it. This is certain, based on our experience. Don't be a hero. Don't go the extra mile. Just do a good job.

8. Avoid apologizing too much.
For most people, when there's a conflict they each take responsibility. They often apologize for their part in it, no matter how small. HCPs often create a lot of conflicts, but when those around them apologize they use it as ammunition against them instead and don't apologize at all themselves. Watch out for this and avoid apologizing or else you will reinforce in their minds that you have done something seriously wrong. (See Chapter 11, under Apology Quicksand.)

9. Pay attention to your fear.
Some HCPs are dangerous. Pay attention to uncomfortable gut feelings; they may be warning signs of trouble ahead. While physical danger is rare, it can occur, as described in Chapter 5, under Violence Concerns. Becoming a target of blame is common with HCPs, who often attack those most trying to help them. You may have rumors spread about you or threats to sue you or blame you for how the case turns out. Get consultation if you are unsure you are facing a threat.

10. Avoid believing your client(s).
Sadly, HCPs say a lot of things that are exaggerations or simply false. They often are not even aware of this. Don't assume that you are getting the full story. Don't make a confrontation out of it; just don't rely heavily on what they tell you. If it's important, ask for verification. If asked to verify what the other says, tell them that you can't know if they are being totally open and honest with each other, such as with financial disclosures and other relationships.

11. Avoid believing stories about other professionals.
High conflict people will often tell you that other people are acting badly, especially other professionals who they claim have treated them poorly. Don't assume that this is true. The others may have set necessary limits on them or realized that they were not being told the truth. Remember that their targets of blame are usually people they are close to and people in authority positions. Professionals are often in both positions, so they get blamed a lot.

12. Avoid becoming isolated in your work with HCPs.
Mediation can be a lonely occupation since most of the work is done alone. When you are working with HCPs, the stress can build up. It

helps to have others who you can debrief with confidentially and use for consultation. But be careful not to complain about your cases to anyone who will listen. Confidentiality is easy to lose track of when you are stressed. Some mediators use consultation groups and professional organizations to stay balanced.

Conclusion

The above is a list of some of the biggest ethical concerns when working with potentially high conflict clients. There are also numerous ethical rules and standards that mediators can consult for any ethical situation, such as those provided by professional organizations, including the Academy of Professional Family Mediators, the Association for Conflict Resolution, the ADR Section of the American Bar Association, and others. Each state also has professional rules and laws that may or may not impact mediators or certain types of mediators. But if you follow these twelve tips, you are much less likely to get into ethical or legal trouble when you work with mediation clients, especially high conflict clients.

CHAPTER 19

Difficult Endings

High conflict people have a difficult time with relationships, especially close relationships and relationships with people in authority positions. As a professional helping with intimate problems in mediation, you are likely to be seen as both an intimate other and someone in authority. Therefore, you should always be prepared for the possibility of an abrupt or otherwise difficult ending. You may go from being seen as a helpful ally to an evil enemy at any time. Several issues are to be anticipated when working with high conflict clients. Here are some tips that can help you deal with them calmly and respectfully:

- Avoid firing your difficult clients
- If you have to stop
- Financial disputes with clients

Avoid Firing Your Difficult Clients

Since high conflict people can be so challenging, mediators often wonder if it is time to end their working relationship—to fire the clients. This is to be discouraged for at least two reasons:

It takes them longer: It is very common for high conflict people to take longer to reach agreements, because they often react emotionally to each new issue before they can respond logically. They also have a hard time with loss, and making decisions usually involves loss—either of money, relationships, or the unrealistic dream of their expectations (the greatest partner, job, team, etc.) If at all possible, it helps to hang in there with them and patiently let them know that you will keep at it as long as they want to—or at least a little longer.

Of course, you should explain that you may be out of ideas and unsure if you can help them further, but you will let them make that decision. Many parties eventually reach agreements and are thankful that the mediator kept working with them. Sometimes it is just the presence of your calm demeanor and steady hand that helps them keep working things through to an agreement.

Abandonment issues: Many high conflict people have a painful history of bad endings, which may go back to early childhood. Each difficult ending may trigger the sense of loss of those earlier traumatic abandonments. If you are the one who ends the working relationship, it may trigger that sense of loss in a way that would not have occurred if you left it up to them to end the relationship. Here is an example:

> *In a divorce mediation case, the parties had been away from mediation for several months and returned to finish the process. But they hit a snag over their biggest asset. Suddenly, the husband stood up, collected his papers, and announced that he was quitting the mediation. The mediator asked if he believed he was at an impasse. He said "Yes." The mediator asked the wife and she said "Yes" as well. The mediator then explained that she would write her Impasse Letter to them, explaining that her mediation file was confidential and that she wouldn't be allowed to talk to any future mediator or lawyers unless they both agreed. She mentioned that they were welcome to return at any time. Then the parties left.*
>
> *A week later, the mediator received an email from the husband asking: "Why did you abandon us?" The mediator had not abandoned them, but that is how it felt to the husband (a likely HCP). Despite inviting them to return to mediation, the husband wrote that it was too late. He also wanted to know where to send a letter of complaint.*

As a result of this experience, the mediator decided to always schedule another session for the few couples that believed they were at an impasse, with the option for them to cancel it just two days in advance if they still felt the need. Over the years, in two or three other similar cases, the parties kept these optional, but scheduled appointments and eventually reached agreements.

If You Have to Stop

In general, with HCPs it is best to avoid blaming them for an unhappy ending, but also avoid blaming yourself. It may be easy to blame the behavior of one or both of them, but don't do that! They will use that as a basis to try to sue you or spread bad reviews on the internet.

But if you say it's your fault it didn't work out, then they will ask why you took their case in the first place. This may be a complicated question and its best to not get into that when you're splitting up.

The best approach is to say that it didn't work out because your styles or goals may have been different. It wasn't a good fit after all. This keeps it out of the blame context. Be as friendly about it as you can, keeping in mind that it is a difficult time for them.

Financial Disputes with Clients

On rare occasion, a disgruntled client won't just fire you, they might demand their money back. This happened to Bill once after he had mediated nearly a thousand divorce cases. Here is the essence of the letter he received from a client who had come late to the mediation session, took a phone call during the session, then left early. Neither party had an attorney at the session.

Dear Mediator:

You met with us on Sept. 9th for our divorce mediation and we scheduled another meeting for Sept. 23rd. We are now canceling that meeting, because both my wife and I (and my attorney) believe that you did not handle our mediation properly. We accomplished nothing in our first meeting. I paid for the mediation session and I would like my money back. Please respond promptly. We have found another mediator who does it correctly.

— Disgruntled Client

The mediator replied with a BIFF Response (brief, informative, friendly, and firm):

Dear Client,

Thank you for your letter expressing your concerns about our mediation session. After doing nearly 1000 divorce mediation cases and teaching a course in mediation at two law schools, I have learned that people have different styles of providing mediation services. I am glad that you have found a mediator that fits for you. Best wishes in completing your divorce.

Sincerely

Mediator[20]

In this case, the mediator could have attached a copy of the Agreement to Mediate, which says that fees are not refundable for services already rendered. However, that would be suggesting the negative (see Chapter 11), which may have made him feel even worse and angrier. Instead, the mediator chose to simply point out how experienced she was and leave it at that. Apparently, the client got the message and never responded again.

The BIFF Response format is designed for communications involving a potentially high conflict person. For more on that method, see Bill's book *BIFF: Quick Responses to High Conflict People, Their Personal Attacks, Hostile Email and Social Media Meltdowns.* This example is taken from this book.

Conclusion

It is realistic and necessary to anticipate the possibility of an unhappy and abrupt ending to working with high conflicts clients in mediation, just like everywhere else. Do not take this personally. Try not to be the one to fire your clients, as this might not be necessary, as they take longer to reach agreements and this may unnecessarily trigger abandonment feelings.

Since HCPs blame their conflicts entirely on the other person, it is not surprising that some of them will want to be refunded for services they have already received, because in their eyes the services were all bad and all the other person's fault. In such a case, a BIFF Response is often the recommended way to go.

CHAPTER 20

The Future of
High Conflict Mediation

High conflict people come from every occupation, income level, ethnic group, and geographic area in the world. They may be approximately ten percent of the adult population and they appear to be increasing.

Yet, over the years, we have learned that high conflict clients need structure, skills, and limits. Rather than needing more opportunities for self-expression of their hurts and grievances about the past, they need more self-restraint so they can focus on learning and using problem-solving skills. When they succeed, they are very pleased with what they have been able to accomplish. Mediation is a process that helps people solve problems together, and mediation designed for high conflict people, such as the *New Ways for Mediation* method, has been very effective from our experience and the reports of many colleagues over the last twelve years.

Ironically, our legal systems promote litigation of disputes, to determine winners and losers, rather than to solve problems and resolve conflicts. While litigation attracts large numbers of high conflict people, it does not help them very much, and tends to escalate and prolong their disputes—with a great cost to the parties and taxpayers financially, and a great cost emotionally to families, workplaces, and communities. However, judicial and legislative leaders worldwide have been figuring this out and there is a strong push today for moving legal disputes out of the courts and into mediation wherever possible.

Unfortunately, the mediation methods of the past have been primarily designed for people who are not high conflict. Instead, they work well with people who are capable of self-reflection about their past deeds, insights about changes they will try to make, and open to hearing each other's emotions with empathy and respect. These methods work well for about 80% of people and, not surprisingly, they are able to resolve most of their disputes out of court. This means that the courts are significantly filled with high conflict cases, many of which include two high conflict parties and many of which include just one high conflict party. In either case, the traditional concepts of justice are misleading and often unhelpful in these cases.

The result is that we now have mediation methods and skills that can help high conflict people resolve their disputes—which will help society at large—if we are willing to use them. This brings us to three tasks which will take sufficient motivation from leaders and ordinary co-workers, family and friends:

1. Require people to use mediation first, before allowing or encouraging them to vent and fight in court, the media, and in groups. Most people reach agreements in mediation, including high conflict people, if they are not allowed to give in to their adversarial urges for a while.

2. Require people to learn skills and make them readily available, such as in pre-mediation coaching or programs, so that they will have the ability to manage their emotions, make and respond to proposals, and manage their own behavior in decision-making and afterwards.

3. Train enough people in mediation methods for high conflict people, so that they can succeed in resolving their disputes much more successfully, quickly and in a long-lasting manner. We believe that *New Ways for Mediation* is one of those methods and is designed to be easy to teach and easy to learn.

We hope that you agree. The world can no longer afford to be preoccupied with high conflict behavior as a spectator sport. It's reached the point where it may threaten all of us. Yet we know what to do and we have the ability to do it.

With all of that said, we want you to know that we have thoroughly enjoyed writing this book and thinking about all of the issues and challenges that we have experienced in learning the tips and tools and method that we have taught you here. We hope you find this helpful.

Appendix A: Outline of
New Ways for Mediation® Method

Stage 1: Establishing the Process

The *New Ways for Mediation* process is simple but needs to be firm from the start. The first stage sets the tone and focuses the parties' expectations on using their skills throughout the process. This stage can take longer than in other mediation formats as the mediator is bonding with the parties through the process of questions and explanations, as well as establishing the mediator has tight control of the process.

WHAT TO COVER

A. Information that you would normally cover in this step – ground rules, housekeeping

B. Explain the Mediation Process

> Describe the Mediation Process Stages
>
> Fundamentals
>
> > You're the Decision-Makers.
> >
> > I have experience, but not advice, with this subject. Think of me as a source of information.
> >
> > You have more flexibility if you agree than a judge or third-party decision maker does.

C. Explain Roles

> My role is to
>
> > Control and guide the process,
> >
> > Stay neutral and not decide who is right or wrong,
> >
> > Educate about options and possible outcomes
>
> Explain clients' role is to
>
> > Ask questions
> >
> > Make their agenda,

Make their proposals,

Make their decisions

Briefly explain making and responding to proposals.

D. Sign any paperwork such as Agreement to Mediate

E. Invite Questions

They usually will have proposals, arguments, and challenges.

Provide information in a matter-of-fact manner and help them resolve initial issues such as who pays (have them make proposals and analyze them if necessary).

Calmly defer their discussion of substantive issues for later stages in the process.

F. Briefly Repeat Description of Process Stages.

TIPS

1. Remind the parties the focus of the process is on the future (not the past).
2. Establish your authority for managing the process and the structure.
3. Explain the process—in as brief and simple terms as you can.
4. Stick to each step. Stop them from diverting you. Stay firm about delaying issues until you have completed this stage.
5. Use proposal process to deal with issues that come up that must be agreed upon (how the mediation will be paid for).
6. Give them hope that this structure usually works.
7. Gently avoid story telling—it usually reinforces emotions and positions.
8. Stay firm about delaying issues (like not wanting to get divorced; full facts about incomes; etc.) until this stage is completed.
9. Don't focus on how they feel—their feelings usually improve as the process moves forward and they can raise their concerns and be heard.
10. Disputes over minor issues may need to be resolved in this step, such as who pays, as they can derail process—but it's a dispute for them to resolve.
11. Encourage proposals for all issues they raise, even from the start.

This helps establish their decision-making.

12. Tell them what options they have; what others have done. This keeps it on their shoulders. Mediator accepts it as important issue, but doesn't solve it.

13. On rare occasions, HCPs won't sign Agreement to Mediate and mediator says can't work without it. Suggest options: discuss with an attorney, think about it, and schedule another appointment; meet with them separately for a few minutes to discuss options.

SCRIPTS

Aspects of Mediation:

"Welcome to mediation. Before we get started, I want to emphasize three key aspects of the mediation process. #1: You folks are the decision-makers. I won't make decisions for you, I won't pressure you to make decisions and you don't have to persuade me of anything. #2: I may have information on the subjects you are trying to decide today, and I am happy to share what knowledge I have about how other people have handled similar issues – but it is all information and not advice. #3: If you are dealing with a court case, it is helpful to know that the courts encourage mediation and will accept almost any out-of-court agreements you make, because you have more flexibility than a judge has so long as you both agree. Do you have any questions about these key aspects of mediation before we proceed?"

Brief Explanation of Proposals Approach:

"The focus of mediation is on the future, so that we will spend most of our time on each of you making proposals and refining your proposals until they can become agreements. I will help you with this process and explain more about this as we go. Also, when you hear a proposal, try to focus on responding simply with a 'Yes,' 'No,' or 'I'll think about.' Again, I will help you with this process. Think of me as responsible for the process and the two of you as responsible for making your decisions. Any questions about any of this?"

Dealing with Hijacks

Calmly insist on addressing any diversionary issues *after* you have explained your mediation process.

"We will get to those types of concerns shortly. First, I have to explain the process to you, so you'll know what to expect and what your part is. This will be very brief. It's what I've found to be the most helpful to do. So, I appreciate your patience. Thanks."

Stage 2: Making Their Agenda

This stage puts responsibility directly on the parties to raise issues and agree on which issues they will discuss, including the order in which they will discuss them. By keeping this responsibility on the parties rather than on the mediator, it builds momentum for them making proposals and joint agreements. The mediator emphasizes that it is the parties' dispute and their joint decisions to be made, which reinforces the expectation that they will be responsible for the outcome, not the mediator.

WHAT TO COVER

A. Initial Thoughts & Questions - Ask for Thoughts and Questions about the decisions they need to make.

> Allow the parties to discuss any appropriate pending issues that were delayed.

> You could suggest questions or simple categories of decisions they will need to make. This way you provide them with a structure for this part.

> Ask for one person to start to go through Thoughts & Questions without interruption, then have the other do so.

>> Thoughts are the person's initial ideas or thoughts about what they would like to see happen with each issue.

>> Questions are a chance for the person to ask the mediator information questions about an issue.

> Avoid anything that opens up the past or emotions.

> Encourage them to take notes if they urgently want to speak, explain listening is hard at first.

B. Answer their Questions - Review basic information about the topics they have raised. The mediator can summarize what each party said and then give basic information on standards that relate to the issues they have raised (almost a mini seminar). For example, in divorce mediation, the mediator can explain the basics of parenting plans, property division, child support and other issues, so that the parties narrow their expectations and get to ask more questions.

Ask them for information that will help them make decisions. By focusing on standards and options before the parties make their proposals, it saves them embarrassment and unrealistic expectations. It also helps the mediator avoid appearing to take sides.

Normalize hearing standards and gathering information as the way to prepare for making proposals. Remind them it will be up to them to make proposals and they can vary from standards. The mediator will need to repeat this information during Stage 3 as it can be confusing.

C. Building Their Agenda – Work with the parties to make their Agenda

Ask them for a proposed list of topics they would like to put on their Agenda.

Get agreement on the topics and order.

These could be the broad categories the mediator already identified, or new issues.

Parties can raise any issue they want to discuss and they can say "No" to any issue they don't want to discuss.

TIPS

1. The mediator encourages each party to look at and speak to the mediator (in the presence of the other party), so the mediator can really concentrate on the party who is speaking. This also discourages sniping comments back and forth, as the parties are not looking at each other and simply reacting to each other. This further trains the parties to take turns and listen without interrupting throughout the process. It is also a time to predict and normalize disagreement – and that disagreements can be resolved.

2. With high conflict people there will be a lot of interrupting during this step, even though they have been instructed not to interrupt. (Remember, unmanaged emotions are common for some

HCPs) It is helpful at this point to show comfort with managing the process and calmly reinforce the benefit of each person speaking thoroughly, so that the mediator can really understand each one's point of view.

3. Don't let these issues become power struggles. Instead, say that you are simply sharing information you believe will help them understand their options and make proposals that can become agreements. Encourage them to seek the advice of separate lawyers or advisors to get more detailed information on what you are generally telling them.

SCRIPTS

Introduction:

"What I'd let to do is get your thoughts in 4 areas of decision-making we are going to discuss today and any questions you may have for me about them. This is often the hardest part of the process because you may hear points of view that you disagree with. That's fine and normal at this stage, as most people start out disagreeing and most people eventually reach agreements in mediation. So, if you have a reaction or idea while the other person is talking, feel free to make a note of anything you wish, so that you can just listen without interrupting. After I hear from each of you, we will make our agenda of what you jointly agree you wish to discuss. You can raise any issue for discussion, and you can say "no" to any issue you do not wish to discuss. Who wants to go first?"

Information:

"You've raised an important subject and here's how it is commonly handled…"

Dealing with questions put over from Stage 1:

"What I'd like to do is get your thoughts and questions in 4 areas of decision-making, so you know what's coming, but first let's address that threshold question you had James…"

Dealing with interruptions:

"This helps me think more effectively of ways that I might help the two of you resolve the problems you want to address today."

"It's normal to feel frustrated at this stage of the process, yet it usually helps each of you in thinking about the proposals that you're going to make and most people eventually reach agreement in this process."

"Listen, folks. Let's all of us try not to make little side comments and let's all of us try not to react to little side comments. Now, where were we?..."

Stage 3: Making Their Proposals

Once there has been a discussion of issues and standards, and the parties have set their agenda priorities, it is time for proposals. This method allows them to present their proposals but then the mediator assists them with understanding the underlying parts, including interests.

In the *New Ways for Mediation* method, the mediator is clearly managing the process with a very direct approach, while not taking any responsibility for the outcome. By taking this highly-structured approach, the mediator actually makes the process simpler and more user friendly for the parties, while also protecting them from each other's (and their own) negative impulses.

By training them in the 3-step proposal method, you get them thinking about the future and picturing solutions to their problems. You avoid getting "hooked" into their helplessness and you can often redirect them into thinking about their future options versus rehashing their positions and complaints about the other.

WHAT TO COVER

A. Ask for questions:

>   Once you are at the first topic in their agenda, ask if they have any questions you can answer about this topic before you hear proposals.

Preparing them for proposals:

>   Briefly explain the proposal-making process.

>   Having a visual reminder of this process on a whiteboard can be extremely helpful.

The mediator ensures the parties have information on standards, approaches or options for resolution before making proposals and continue doing this throughout.

Guide the parties through making proposals:

MAKE A PROPOSAL: Encourage the parties to make a proposal (WHO, WHAT, WHEN, WHERE avoid WHY) on the topic they chose.

ASK QUESTIONS: Encourage the other party to ask at least two questions about the proposal. This encourages thinking, rather than reacting. These questions should not include WHY questions, as they usually are criticisms. The proposing party must answer those questions as matter of factly as possible. The mediator should ask some questions as this demonstrates an objective search for solutions and discourages parties from quickly saying "No" to each other's proposals and slows down rapid-fire rejection and appearance of impasse that often occurs with HCPs.

RESPOND: Help the other party to respond with "Yes, No or I'll think about it." If he or she says "I'll think about it," ask how much time they will need (such as 5 minutes, a day, a week).

If the responding party says "No," then it is their turn to make a proposal back.

TIPS

Help the parties gather information about proposals. The mediator can suggest information they could gather, remind the parties of the default standards for a given issue, or provide more detailed information about the law or alternatives others have used. If the mediator suggests options, they should try to suggest 3 options.

DEALING WITH INTERESTS

The mediator can deconstruct proposals to identify for the parties the interests that are important to them. Highlighting interests can be helpful, however if the mediator spends too much time focusing on interests it can start an unnecessary fight because:

HCPs have resistance to the idea of interests and analyzing them.

They don't think they have interests; they just think they are right.

SCRIPTS

Explaining the Proposal-making process:

"Proposals are the building blocks of agreement. After you make proposals, ask questions which will help lead us toward new proposals and new responses until you have an agreement.

When we make proposals, we use a 3-step process, which keeps it simple:

1. First, one of you makes a proposal, containing Who will do What, When and Where.

2. Then, the other asks questions about the proposal—such as when it starts, what your part is in the plan—which are also Who, What, When and Where questions. Please don't ask Why questions, because those are usually criticisms in disguise. Then the proposer answers those questions.

3. Then, the other says 'Yes,' 'No,' or 'I'll think about it.'

This keeps it very focused on what to do, rather than talking about the past, who to blame, etc. And if the responder says No, then the responder makes a proposal. We go back and forth until we develop a good plan—an agreement.

Any questions about that?"

Intervening when a party wants to respond to a proposal immediately:

"Hang on, Dan. Don't respond yet to Emily's proposal until we really understand it. We want to make sure we're absorbing all the parts of her proposal, which may help me and you two to refine your proposals until you are ready to reach an agreement. Sometimes a proposal itself is not agreed to, but it helps us find another solution that will work for you both. So, Emily, tell me what it would look like if your proposal was put into action. What would your picture be? What you would do, what Dan would do and anyone else involved?"

"I have some questions also, which will help me to help you understand where you might find room for agreement."

Inviting a party to respond to a proposal:

"What are your questions for Emily about her proposal? Do you think you understand it pretty clearly? Ok, then what are your thoughts about it? Would this be a 'Yes, I can do it!' 'No, I won't do it.' or 'I'll think about it.' And if you want to think about it, when do you think you'll have an answer for her? And if your answer is a "No," then of course I'll be asking you next what your proposal would be."

If a party says their proposal has to be accepted and it's not "Just a Proposal":

"That's fine, you might be right. It might become your final agreement. But it really helps to have a full discussion of several proposals before reaching a final agreement, if you want it to last." People usually accept that, because the proposal hasn't been rejected and it has actually been cast in a positive light.

Avoiding putting pressure on a party:
"This is all information; it is not advice."

"I won't pressure you to make a proposal, and I won't pressure you to accept a proposal."

If you reach an impasse and none of the above is effective:

Tell them you are out of ideas, if you are, but you will keep working with them.

Ask if they would like to stop for today and set a future meeting.

Stage 4: Making Their Decisions

When they have reached initial agreement on their decisions, the mediator should make sure to go over the details that will be necessary to implement these decisions. This may include issues that the parties have been "thinking about." It usually involves several edits of a written agreement involving lawyers and other advisers. High conflict people can resolve most of their disputes, but they can often take twice or three times as long to reach final agreements. Even though HCPs can do logical problem-solving with professionals, they often go home and become upset again as they interpret their agreement in negative relationship terms (feeling abandoned, disrespected, ignored, dominated). When they are around their reasonable advisers again their tentative agreements look reasonable again. This can go back and forth several times until the agreement is finished.

WHAT TO COVER

Prepare draft written agreements for the parties to review and comment on.

Avoid "hammering out" agreements—the parties will often undermine this effort.

Be prepared to calmly repeat information, answer questions and deal with upset over your drafting.

Take a neutral position about making edits and changes.

Build breaks into this step to allow the parties to get advice from their lawyers and other advisers. Consider making contact with the adviser so they have a balanced perspective on the draft agreement.

Remain connected with the parties throughout this step. This usually means maintaining face-to-face contact through this step.

TIPS

1. Remind yourself, "the mediator is responsible for the process and their standard of professional care, but is not responsible for the outcome."

2. If a party tries to pass responsibility for solving issues with the draft on to the mediator say, "It's up to you! To the two of you!"

Appendix B:
Client Pre-Mediation Handout

If you're preparing for a mediation to solve any type of problem, it helps to know about 4 Big Skills™ that can help you during the mediation process. Most mediations involve a mediator who has been trained to stay neutral and help the participants make their own decisions. The mediator is in charge of the process and the participants are in charge of making proposals and making decisions about the issues at hand. Sometimes people try to persuade the mediator to take sides, but the mediator is supposed to be very careful to stay neutral and to help the parties make their own decisions. The following 4 skills can help.

1. Managed Emotions

Talking about unresolved issues can be emotionally upsetting. However, it is possible to manage your own emotions by anticipating upsetting moments and preparing for them. Don't be surprised if you feel frustrated or angry upon hearing different points of view, hearing proposals you don't like, and having to think of alternatives. Remember that most conflicts are resolved through this process of talking and listening and creating solutions. Prepare yourself to deal with any possible difficult moments.

How can you help yourself stay calm? One of the best techniques is to *memorize short encouraging statements* that you can tell yourself as you are going through the process, such as:

PATIENCE:
- The agreement at the end is all that matters
- Sometimes it takes a while, but an agreement is usually reached
- With high conflict emotions it usually takes longer, but agreements can still be reached.

DON'T TAKE IT PERSONALLY:
- Personal attacks are not about me – they're about the person who lacks self-control.

- I don't have to defend myself or prove myself – I'm already okay as a person.
- We can disagree about the past – reaching an agreement about the future is what matters.

2. Flexible Thinking

A big focus of mediation and other settlement methods is making proposals. It helps to prepare proposals for each issue you are trying to resolve or plan to raise in the mediation. That way you don't get stuck in "all-or-nothing thinking" and can avoid just getting upset when your first proposal isn't immediately accepted. Any concern about the past can be turned into a proposal about the future.

It can help to prepare two proposals on any issue that you or the other person is likely to raise, so that you don't get stuck if your first proposal is not accepted right away. You can make a list of issues and then write two proposals for how you would like to see each one get resolved.

During a mediation, it is common for the mediator to ask for proposals (ideas, options, suggestions, solutions, etc.) at some point. It can help to think of making proposals in three steps:

1. **Make a proposal:** This usually will include WHO will do WHAT, WHEN and WHERE.

2. **Ask questions:** When would this begin? What would my part be? Can you give me a detailed picture of how you see this working? Then the proposer answers the questions.

3. **Respond:** Simply say "Yes." "No." Or "I'll think about it." If Yes, then write it up. If No, then calmly say you disagree, then focus on making a new proposal. The other person needs to make a proposal, so both people are thinking of ideas. If its "I'll think about it," then find out how long they need to think or agree on a time limit.

This approach avoids arguing unnecessarily over a proposal itself, since what really matters is coming to an agreement. Just make a proposal, ask questions, and respond. It can help to practice this with someone before a mediation, such as with a pre-mediation coach.

You can also use this method on your own even without a mediator, before or after a mediation. But wait until you have a mediator if you get stuck. Avoid getting into an argument or you'll both stay stuck.

3. Moderate Behaviors

Mediation is a structured process, to help people think of reasonable solutions to problems, even when they are upset. Therefore, there are several ground rules in most mediations. It helps to think about them in advance and remind yourself to follow them, including:

A. Don't interrupt while the other person is speaking. Instead, make notes to remind yourself of any ideas that pop up while he or she is talking. Then you can raise them when appropriate.

B. Treat everyone with respect. This means avoiding insulting comments, raising your voice or pointing fingers. These behaviors often trigger defensiveness in the other person. Instead, you want everyone to stay calm and rational, in order to focus on solving the problems you came to discuss. Speaking respectfully goes a long way toward reaching agreements that will work and last over time.

C. Use "I" statements. These are sentences that start with "I feel…" or "I prefer…" or "I have another idea…" Avoid "You" statements, such as "You always…" or "You never…" "You" statements tend to trigger defensiveness in the other person, which will make it harder to reach an agreement. Just use "I" statements to convey your own perspective, rather than assumptions or criticisms of the other person's perspective. Remember, all you need to do is to reach an agreement. You don't need to try to change the other person's way of thinking (which is unlikely anyway).

D. Ask to take a break, if necessary. Avoid just getting up and walking out. Ask for a break, so that everyone can stop for a few minutes. Mediation is more flexible than a court hearing or arbitration. Taking breaks can help you earn respect – rather than resentment if you rush out – and can help you calm down if you're upset. It's also fine to take a break to get advice from a lawyer, friend or other advisor before you make final agreements. Just ask for some time to do so – either a few minutes, or several days or weeks if necessary. Mediators generally do not pressure you to make final decisions at the same time as you first discuss an issue.

4. Check Yourself

From time to time, ask yourself if you are using these skills. It's easy to forget in the middle of discussing problems or upsetting issues. The mediator will try to help everyone in the mediation stay calm and focus on understanding problems and finding solutions. Just think about these four skills before the mediation and during the mediation, and you may do very well.

Appendix C: Mediation Demonstration PowerPoint Slides

The following PowerPoint slides accompany the 3-hour demonstration video of Bill Eddy mediating a variety of high conflict situations in a divorce mediation with "Dawn and Skip." This recorded video is available on demand (with an introductory 75-minute recorded seminar) on the High Conflict Institute website: **www.highConflictInstitute.com** under "training."

Appendix D: Role-Play

New Ways for Mediation®
More Structure, More Skills and Less Stress
for Potentially High-Conflict Cases

[These slides accompany the 3-hour demonstration video of a divorce mediation using this method available on www.HighConflictInstitute.com]

A 3-hour Demonstration of
Issues and Interventions with
Bill Eddy, Mediator

1

About This Demonstration

This mediation demonstration is performed with actors portraying behaviors and issues from real cases which are potentially common in divorce mediation.

The purpose is to demonstrate the New Ways for Mediation method rather than to be a dramatic production. To save time, the parties act more like ordinary people, with occasional outbursts. Yet the method presented has been used to manage highly- confrontational clients who repeatedly challenge the mediator and each other. Comments are made about managing additional high-conflict issues throughout.

There is a Table of Contents and Issue Index (2) at the end.

2

New Ways for Mediation
Structure

Stage 1:	Orientation and Agreement to Mediate
Stage 2:	The Parties Make Their Agenda
Stage 3:	The Parties Make Their Proposals
Stage 4:	The Parties Make Their Decisions

3

Stage 1

Orientation and Agreement to Mediate:

Pre-Mediation Coaching – Each person individually

Joint session – Explaining Process, Establishing Roles

Signing the Agreement to Mediate

4

Discussion

Pre-Mediation Coaching
- This is an optional activity
  - depends on cost and time available
  - can accomplish some of this at first session
- Opportunity to bond with each client
- Opportunity to explain process to anxious clients; give **4 skills** to use in mediation
- Opportunity to explore any power imbalance issues and inappropriateness for mediation

5

High-Conflict Parties (HCPs)

Pre-Mediation Coaching
- HCPs are often not obvious at first to mediator
- Opportunity to establish control of process; (HCPs often try to control process)
- Establish mediator's authority by doing most talking at first; block storytelling – just tends to reinforce HCP's emotions and positions
- Establish clients' responsibility for problem-solving: asking questions, setting agenda, making proposals and making decisions

6

High-Conflict Issues

Pre-Mediation Coaching
- Establish your neutral role
- Whatever issues raised (such as *not wanting divorce; drinking problem*), approach as the parties' dilemma and give information about options, structures for resolving it
- Emphasize having them ask you questions, rather than you asking them lots of content questions – it will help them work harder and be more invested in process & decisions

7

Stage 1

Orientation and Agreement to Mediate:

Pre-Mediation Coaching – Each person individually

Joint session – Explaining Process, Establishing Roles

Signing the Agreement to Mediate

8

Stage 1

Orientation and Agreement to Mediate:

Pre-Mediation Coaching – Each person individually

Joint session – Explaining Process, Establishing Roles

Signing the Agreement to Mediate

9

Discussion

Joint Session –
   Explaining Process; establishing roles
- Keep focus on information – giving, gathering, offering to answer questions
- Mediator's role as a guide
- Keep focus on the process until Agreement to Mediate signed (hold off on issue of not getting divorced, income disputes, etc.)

10

High-Conflict Parties

Joint Session –

Explaining Process; establishing roles

- HCPs interrupt a lot; gently avoid storytelling – it usually reinforces emotions and positions
- Stay firm about delaying issues (like not wanting divorce; full facts about incomes; etc.) until Agreement to Mediate is signed
- Remember, its up to them how they resolve each issue – even from the start
- Don't focus on how they feel – their feelings usually improve as the process moves forward and they can raise their concerns and be heard

11

High-Conflict Issues

Joint Session – Explaining Process; establishing roles

- Disputes over minor issues, such as who pays, can derail process – but it's a dispute for them to resolve.
- Encourage proposals for all issues they raise – even from the start. Helps establish their decision-making.
- Tell them what options they have; what others have done. This keeps it on their shoulders. Mediator accepts it as important issue – but doesn't solve it.
- On rare occasion, HCPs won't sign and mediator simply says can't work without it – suggests options: discuss with an attorney; think about it and schedule another appointment; meet with them separately for a few minutes to discuss options

12

Stage 2

The Parties Make Their Agenda:

Ask for thoughts and questions in main categories of decision-making

Give basic information about the topics they raised

Ask them what issues they would like to put on their Agenda for today's meeting and where to start

13

Introducing Stage 2

Ask for thoughts and questions in main categories of decision-making

- Need to discuss any pending issues delayed until Agreement to Mediate was signed
- Give them categories of decisions they will need to make (parenting, support, property)
- Ask for one to go through thoughts & questions *without interruption*; then have the other do so
- Encourage them to take notes if they urgently want to speak; explain listening is hard at first

14

High-Conflict Issues

Ask for thoughts, questions in main categories

- At this stage, help them not respond to each other's issues, but raise their own points of view (to minimize defensiveness)
- Give brief explanations when conflicts arise – helps keep peace while responding to concerns
- Avoid disciplinary comments about how they're behaving – just keep focus on the future and tell them to think of questions to ask and proposals they'll make – and can take notes while listening

15

High-Conflict Parties

Ask for thoughts and questions in main categories

- HCPs have a hard time hearing the other party's thoughts; uncontrollable interrupting can occur –
- Sometimes allow interruptions if other party seems to respond positively (they may realize this is the only way it will work)
- Stop angry attacks quickly; they can't handle them; stay calm and they often calm down
- Give Empathy and Respect for their concerns
- Let them know they'll be heard soon;
- Ask if they can proceed or need a break: it's up to them (but mediator can always impose a break too)

16

Stage 2

The Parties Make Their Agenda:

Ask for thoughts and questions in main categories of decision-making

Give basic information about the topics they raised

Ask them what issues they would like to put on their Agenda for today's meeting and where to start

17

Discussion

Give basic information about the topics they raised

- By providing basic information about legal and other standards early in the process, you aren't identified with one party's proposals later in the process
- Standards provided in this mediation are based on California law – each state has slightly different standards; laws change so this is not legal advice
- Sometimes the information they hear varies from agreements they have already proposed or made
- Since the parties don't have lawyers involved up to now, its important that they get the legal standards from the mediator

18

High-Conflict Issues

Give basic information about the topics they raised

- Each of these issues has lots of stuff to argue about
- Normalize hearing standards and gathering information as the way to prepare for making proposals
- Keep reminding them that it will be up to them to make proposals and they can vary from standards
- But keep giving them standards before discussions
- Repetition can be helpful, as this all can be confusing

19

High-Conflict Parties

Give basic information about the topics they raised

- During this presentation of information, HCPs often start making their demands or stating their positions; just help them stay calm as they hear unsettling info.
- Don't let them jab at each other too much, like you would in a normal mediation – HCPs can't handle it.
- By getting this info out there early, it helps them become more realistic, as HCPs tend to have extreme views of the standards – favorable or unfavorable.

("Fathers have no rights!")

("I'm getting the f---ing house!") Etc.

20

Stage 2

The Parties Make Their Agenda

Ask for thoughts and questions in main categories of decision-making

Give basic information about the topics they raised

Ask them what issues they would like to put on their Agenda for today's meeting and where to start

21

Stage 3

The Parties Make Their Proposals

Help them make proposals on the topic they chose

Help them respond with "Yes, No or I'll think about it"

Give them standards that may help along the way

Help them ask each other questions about proposals

22

Discussion

Help them make proposals on the topic they chose

- Help them finish a proposal before other responds

- Help them avoid arguing about issues they agree on

23

Stage 3

The Parties Make Their Proposals

Help them make proposals on the topic they chose

Help them respond with "Yes, No or I'll think about it"

Give them standards that may help along the way

Help them ask each other questions about proposals

24

Discussion

Help them respond with "Yes, No or I'll think about it"

- Keep them on track about responding, rather than drifting into criticisms

- Keep arguments from escalating; don't just watch them arguing; but stay calm

- But don't take a position on any issue - stay focused on process of proposal-making and responding

25

Stage 3

The Parties Make Their Proposals

Help them make proposals on the topic they chose

Help them respond with "Yes, No or I'll think about it"

Give them standards that may help along the way

Help them ask each other questions about proposals

26

Discussion

Give them standards that may help along the way
- This helps you keep the focus on information and away from defensive reacting

- This often reassures one or both parties that their concerns are protected under the law

- This often helps them narrow their proposals

- They often find other people's solutions helpful

27

Stage 3

The Parties Make Their Proposals

Help them make proposals on the topic they chose

Help them respond with "Yes, No or I'll think about it"

Give them standards that may help along the way

Help them ask each other questions about proposals

28

Discussion

Help them ask each other questions about proposals

• Encourage them to provide information to each other

• Encourage them to ask questions of each other

• Encourage them to make a new proposal, if they have a different viewpoint

• Encourage them to take time to think about proposals

29

Child Support

Use the same overall approach:
• Provide standard information

• Encourage them to provide information to each other

• Encourage them to ask questions of each other

• Encourage them to make proposals

• Encourage them to take time to think about proposals

30

Alcohol and Drug Use

• Can be an issue regarding parenting plan.

• Give information about local standards.

• Treat it as another problem for the parties to solve, unless both parties appear to be putting the children at risk.

• One approach is having an assessment done to see if there is a problem or not with alcohol and/or drugs – using an objective outside evaluator.

• Terms can go into their overall Agreement – subject to their agreement to do that.

31

Discussion

• This session demonstrated several high-conflict moments, however for demonstration purposes the couple did not remain "high-conflict" and reached agreements fairly easily.

• High-conflict couples often take all-or-nothing positions on the same issues and it may take several sessions to resolve certain issues – the mediator usually doesn't know which these will be.

• Sometimes the high-conflict issues are very minor (furniture division, who gets the camcorder, etc.) and sometimes major (custody, spousal support).

• The same basic methods are used over and over again to manage the process, but not the decisions.

32

Last Session

This session addresses:

• Domestic violence threats
• Restraining orders
• Property division: Court forms; Family Business; retirements; furniture; cars; etc.
• Debts, including credit cards
• Child alienation
• and other issues

33

3 Types
Domestic Violence

1. Controlling violence
   • Constant fear; violent person usually denies it
   • Tends to repeat and escalate after separation
2. Situational couple violence
   • Both people engage in pushing, shoving
   • Usually stops when stop living together
3. Separation-based violence
   • Sometimes 1-2 incidents, threats at separation
   • Sometimes when surprised about end of relationship
   • Usually doesn't continue after separation is clear

34

Discussing Domestic Violence

Since there is a wide range of cases of D. V., the mediator must assess whether it is safe to even meet with the parties together and discuss this issue openly.

This exact incident occurred several years ago, which remained resolved throughout the rest of the case. The mediation discussion "contained" the incident and calmed the conflict.

Generally, I have mediated cases with D. V. – some with restraining orders already in place, others not – and with proper precautions they have been very productive (arriving and leaving separately; meeting in separate rooms; requiring attorneys to be present; etc.).

35

Discussing Child Alienation

Take no assumptions approach – educate both parents.

Can put in agreement: "Neither parent shall make disparaging remarks about the other parent in the presence of the children, nor allow others to do so."

But more important to have parents watch out for the intense emotions they may accidently expose the children to.

36

Stage 4
The Parties Make Their Decisions

Throughout the process mediator made notes of their decisions.

Writing up the agreement terms may be a short or long process – it can take weeks or months, with many edits, but it's always up to them.
The mediator doesn't pressure them; simply keeps using same process.

Explain (and prepare yourself for) changes and new proposals that often come up when reviewing the Agreement ("Marital Settlement Agreement" – MSA).

Recommend reviewing it with separate lawyers, while reminding them that they are the decision-makers.

Explain how to make future decisions–return to mediation, etc.

37

Final Comments

- This couple was not a very high-conflict couple, but had high-conflict moments. Therefore, it's good to know that you can use this approach with any case: Mediator guides the parties, engaging them with more responsibility for:

1. Asking questions
2. Making agenda
3. Making proposals
4. Making decisions

38

Complex Issues

- This case did not address complex issues, such as hidden assets and income, bitter custody disputes, valuing a family business and retirement plans, etc.

- Yet you can use same approach – educate the parties about their alternatives; keep burden on the parties to gather information; help them engage appropriate experts – get expert opinions or invite the experts into the mediation process

39

Lawyers

- This case did not involve lawyers in the mediation sessions. However, in high-conflict cases that are really at an impasse, I encourage (sometimes require – such as in D.V. cases) that the parties bring lawyers with them.

- I strongly encourage my clients to get consultation with separate lawyers, but I don't require it (some mediators do). About 2/3 of my cases don't have lawyers at all, which is why I spend so much time educating the parties about legal "information" and options.

40

Problem-Solving

- This case ended with the parties reaching agreements fairly easily. This actually happens in many of my high-conflict cases, once the parties have really calmed down and accepted the divorce, realities of support, realities of property division and accepted the structured mediation process - which does not reinforce outbursts and efforts to control or dominate the other person.
- However, in truly high-conflict cases, they cannot say much (if anything) positive about the other person, like this couple did (a sign they do not have high-conflict personalities – just moments).

41

Structure and Stress

- As this mediation demonstration shows, the 4-Stage structure of "New Ways for Mediation" is a foundation for the process and helps the mediator maintain control. But it moves back and forth based on the agenda items and the behavior of the parties.
- By having this structure in mind – and the clear roles of the mediator and the parties – I find that I am less stressed and that the parties are less stressed than with most less-structured approaches I have seen and used in the past.

42

Table of Contents

43

Index: Explaining Key Issues

44

Index: Managing Controversies

45

Further Information

For further information or training in
New Ways for Mediation®

www.HighConflictInstitute.com

46

Appendix D:
Role-Play Practice Scenarios

Workplace Mediation Role-Play #1: Family Issues

Participants:
- One workplace mediator
- One high conflict employee (Alex)
- One stressed (not-high conflict) supervisor (Robin)

Meeting jointly as much as possible

Purpose:
- Conduct a preparation session with each party.
- Conduct joint mediation session.

Problem Scenario:
- Alex is a clerk and has worked in the same office for 12 years and used to be a great worker, but their performance has deteriorated dramatically in the last year.
- Alex is a single parent and has been going through a nasty divorce for the past ten years. At the present time, Alex has two teenage children at home, a daughter, who is 16, and a 13-year-old boy. Alex's ex does not pay child support on a regular basis and this leaves Alex as the sole earner as over the years. Alex and the kids cannot depend on them for any support.
- Robin, the supervisor, approached Alex about their work habits and the negative impact their behavior is having on colleagues who cannot focus on their work and clarified that they expect things to improve. Alex became extremely defensive and refused to take any responsibility for her/his behavior. The discussion ended in yelling, on both sides, and Alex accusing Robin of harassment.
- Robin tells their manager that managing Alex's behavior and the impact on other people is taking up 80% of their time.

At the encouragement of the manager, both Robin and Alex have agreed to attend mediation.

Instructions for the Mediator

Conduct individual preparation sessions with each party and then one joint mediation session.

Preparation Sessions

- Build Rapport with the client.
- Walk the client through the Pre-Mediation Handout (see Appendix B).
- Gain commitment to proceed.

Joint Session (Follow the *New Ways for Mediation* Method (see Appendix A)

- Start the session by structuring the process:
    - Explain your role as in charge of guiding the process.
    - Explain their role as making proposals and decisions.
    - Explain that process is not guaranteed, but often succeeds even when parties upset.
    - Explain how the session will be structured:
        - Focus is on the future and decisions about the future,
        - Teach them how to make proposals,
        - Teach them how to respond to proposals.
    - Ask for their initial thoughts and questions about decisions they need to make.
- Help them make an agenda; have them decision first two topics; who goes first.
- Throughout mediation give lots of encouragement and education. Remind them to make proposals when they slip into criticisms. Reinforce small successes. Offer 3 alternatives if needed.
- Try to get a complete agreement on their issues.

Instructions for Alex

You should play Alex as a person who is worn down by the nasty divorce over past 10 years and you show the following high conflict traits:

- A drive to be the center of attention, because of a fear of being ignored,
- Theatrical and dramatic, with shifting emotions, but few facts and little focus,

- Exaggerating events,
- Difficulty focusing on tasks or making decisions.

Lately your daughter has been giving you many problems. She is constantly skipping school; her marks are dropping and now she has informed you that she has a 19-year-old boyfriend (who is a high school drop-out and does not work). The ex blames you for your daughter's behavior. Your Ex is a no good, lazy, piece of work and you don't know how they manipulated you into marrying them.

At work, you dread when your phone rings, because you know it is the school calling to inform you that your daughter has not shown up for school again. The teachers are e-mailing you at work regarding her current grades. It has become so overwhelming for you that you cannot seem to function at work. You have always been a good, reliable worker and you feel that your supervisor should cut you some slack as you are doing the best you can.

The supervisor has approached you on your work habits and has made it very clear that they expect things to improve. You tried to explain your situation to them in hopes of getting some understanding or support, but they were unsympathetic to your situation and as a result, the rest of the conversation did not go well and they started "yelling at you to shape up or you would lose your job". When you think about how uncaring your supervisor is, you get overwhelmed emotionally and start to cry. You think your supervisor wants to get rid of you.

You co-workers know what is going on at home, as the school keeps phoning you during work hours. You have to talk to someone, so you often chat with people at work about how stressful the whole situation is and what a messed-up daughter and crappy Ex you have.

Also, the stress has been very overwhelming to the point where you are losing sleep, especially because you are staying up late waiting for her to come home, if she even does come home.

You are open to collaborative approaches, but you see this as once sided, the supervisor is out to get you and you are just trying to do your job. Explain that no matter what you do, it gets turned on you as though you are the problem, and so the only explanation is the supervisor is trying to get rid of you and you don't know why.

Your friend recommended a mediation, but you do not believe that your supervisor is willing to listen. However, you see the mediator as a possible advocate for you, and you hope, in the mediation, they will tell the supervisor to stop harassing you and that you are doing your best.
Your needs/concerns:
- Financial/support concerns
- Daughter's behavior: concerned for her welfare/safety
- Work: Keep your job—it is the only thing keeping you sane (but perhaps you need a couple of weeks leave to focus on family issues and get your head straight),
- You are open to seeing a counsellor, but things are so crazy you haven't had time to call one and wouldn't even know where to start finding one.
- Desire for support from supervisor

Instructions for the Supervisor (Robin)
You are the supervisor of a clerical section and you have a very difficult employee, Alex, on your hands. You are exhausted from supervising a person who creates drama wherever they go, at work and at home. Alex consumes about 80% of your and others time with their attention seeking, and self-absorbed behavior.
1. Alex has worked for the organization for 12 years and used to be a great worker but her/his performance has deteriorated dramatically in the last year.
2. Alex is a single parent and has been going through a nasty divorce for the past ten years. At the present time, Alex has two teenage children at home, a daughter, who is 16, and a 13-year-old boy. Alex's ex does not pay child support on a regular basis and this leaves Alex as the sole earner as over the years. Alex and the kids cannot depend on the ex for any support.
3. You approached Alex about their work habits and the negative impact their behavior is having on colleagues who cannot focus on their work and clarified that they expect things to improve. Alex became extremely defensive and refused to take any responsibility for their behavior. The conversation ended in Alex yelling and accusing you of harassing her.

You have agreed to attend a mediation and hope it can help fix this, but you are skeptical and think you likely will have to try and use progressive discipline to remedy the situation. However, that could be at least a one-year long process with a lot of conflict.

Needs/Concerns:

- Productive team
- Be seen as a skilled supervisor by your boss and the team
- You are open to being flexible, so long as you are not taken advantage of and that key deadlines and deliverables are met.
- Understand better what is going on for Alex – you do want to help.

Workplace Mediation Role-Play #2: Accounting Problems

Participants:
- One workplace mediator
- One high conflict employee (Riley)
- One Union Representative (Attends the preparation session with Riley) – there are no confidential instructions for this character
- One stressed (not high conflict) supervisor (Addison)

Meeting jointly as much as possible

Purpose:
- Conduct a preparation session with each party.
- Conduct joint mediation session.

Problem Scenario:

This is an administration office with different sections – finance and records. Riley works in finance with 6 other employees. Riley has divided the section into camps, those that support them, those that hate Riley and those that have no interest in the conflict. Riley feels victimized by two women (Rachel and Marge) in the office – telling everyone they are out to get Riley. Riley has convinced two other employees in the office of Robin's case, and they have angrily defended Robin to their coworkers and the supervisor. Rachel and Marge tell the supervisor (Addison), that Riley takes things too personally. Rachel is friends with Riley's ex-spouse, in fact they all used to be friends, when Riley and their ex-spouse were together, but now Riley is upset that Rachel is still friends and tells everyone they are having an affair. Rachel has responded by yelling at Riley in front of everyone in the office. Riley burst into tears and left the office for the day, without speaking to the supervisor.

Addison, the supervisor, called Riley into their office the next morning and was quite frustrated with Riley's behavior. Now Riley is looking at bringing forward a complaint against Addison for harassment/bullying. Riley's Union Advisor has convinced Riley to attempt a mediation process instead.

Instructions for Workplace Mediator

Further Background:

You have some additional background information from the Manager you have connected with and from the intake someone else on your team did.

The Manager responsible for the office says the supervisor (Addison) is effective but avoids conflict and has been trying to deal with Riley by staying on their good side. Riley has resorted to trying to catch the other two women making mistakes and then reports it to the supervisor. The supervisor has responded by asking Riley only to report errors of a serious nature (clear accounting violations). Riley has reported 3 in the last week. Addison decided to try being direct with Riley about their work habits and the negative impact their behavior is having on colleagues who cannot focus on their work and said things had to improve. Riley became extremely defensive and refused to take any responsibility for their behavior. The conversation ended in Riley yelling and accusing Addison of harassing them.

Instructions:

Conduct individual preparation sessions with each party and then one joint mediation session.

Preparation Sessions

- Build Rapport with the client.
- Walk the client through the Pre-Mediation Handout (see Appendix B).
- Gain commitment to proceed.

Joint Session (Follow the *New Ways for Mediation*® Method (see Appendix A)

- Start the session by structuring the process:
    - Explain your role as in charge of guiding the process.
    - Explain their role as making proposals and decisions.
    - Explain that process is not guaranteed, but often succeeds even when parties upset.
    - Explain how the session will be structured:
        - Focus is on the future and decisions about the future,

Teach them how to make proposals,

Teach them how to respond to proposals.

Ask for their initial thoughts and questions about decisions they need to make.

Help them make an agenda; have them decision first two topics; who goes first.

Throughout mediation give lots of encouragement and education. Remind them to make proposals when they slip into criticisms. Reinforce small successes. Offer 3 alternatives if needed.

Try to get a complete agreement on their issues.

Confidential information for Riley (Employee)

Riley is a person with the following high conflict traits:

- A fear of being abandoned which results in clinging behavior and manipulation
- Seeking revenge and vindication when they feel abandoned
- Dramatic mood swings, with extreme positive then negative views on people
- Sudden and intense anger, even at minor incidents

Guidance on how to approach the preparation session with the Mediator:

When starting off the discussion – say you were told by a friend the "mediator" would help them and that you are the best mediator used by the organization. At the same time, you are fearful of mediation, saying the supervisor is out to get you and you are just trying to do your job. Explain that no matter what you do, it gets turned on you as though you are the problem, and so the only explanation is the supervisor is trying to get rid of you and is on Rachel and Marge's side. Your supervisor recently got very angry with you and in a meeting told you that all of the problems in the office were all your fault and that if you didn't stop being mean to Rachel and Marge, your supervisor was going to get you fired! You are totally confused as the supervisor asked you to watch co-workers and you were never told about any problems on your side. Behave as though you see the mediator as a rescuer – say you are looking for them to protect you. Seem innocent and naïve, you don't understand the rules and rely on them for advice and to look out for you – they are the experts! However, if the mediator suggests your behavior might be part of the problem, quickly become highly emotional and critical of the mediator.

Your Union Advisor has persuaded you to attend the Mediation and you have agreed to give it an honest effort as you feel very supported by your Union Advisor and know they will protect you.

However up front, you want the supervisor to acknowledge they made a mistake and that they want to fix things.

Needs/Concerns:

- Be left alone by Rachel and Marge so you can focus on your work,
- You really want Rachel to stop talking to you about your Ex and what they are up to.
- Be included socially with the other staff,
- Be respected and accepted by your supervisor,
- Keep your job.

For the purposes of the role-play, you can be disruptive at points but overall, please cooperate with the mediator's efforts to prepare with you and to guide you through the structure in the subsequent mediation process.

Confidential information for Addison (Supervisor)

You are the supervisor of a clerical section and you have an extremely difficult employee, Riley, on your hands. You are exhausted from supervising a person who creates drama wherever they go, at work and at home. Riley consumes about 80% of your and others' time with her attention seeking and self-absorbed behavior.

1. Riley has worked the organization for 12 years and you have supervised them for the last six months. It has been challenging from the outset and you realize the previous supervisor did not address some difficult behavioral issues. Overall, Riley is competent at the actual work tasks, it is their attitude and behavior that are the problem.

2. You are a relatively new supervisor and are finding this situation very challenging. You don't really like conflict and have been trying to deal with Riley by staying on their good side. Riley seems to be trying to catch Marge and Rachel making mistakes and then

reports these to you. You had become frustrated with Riley's constant interruptions over small issues and thought that you could stop it by saying you were only wanting to know errors of a serious nature (clear accounting violations). Riley has reported 3 in the last week and now you realize your direction to Riley has only further escalated the situation.

3. You decided to try being direct with Riley about their work habits and the negative impact their behavior is having on colleagues who cannot focus on their work and clarified that they expect things to improve. Riley became extremely defensive and refused to take any responsibility for their behavior. The conversation ended in Riley yelling and accusing you of harassing them.

You have agreed to attend a mediation and hope it can help fix this but you are skeptical and think you likely will have to try and use progressive discipline to remedy the situation. However, that could be at least a one-year long process with a lot of conflict.

Needs/Concerns:

- Productive team
- Be seen as a skilled supervisor by your boss and the team
- You are open to being flexible, as long as you are not taken advantage of and that key deadlines and deliverables are met.
- Understand better what is going on for Riley – you do want to help.

For the purposes of the role-play, please cooperate with the mediator's efforts to prepare with you and to guide you through the structure in the subsequent mediation process.

Divorce Mediation: Structuring Dawn and Skip

Participants:

- One family mediator
- Two angry clients
- Meeting jointly as much as possible

Purpose:

- To practice not getting emotionally hooked by an angry client
- To practice giving structure and small skills to clients

Problem Scenario:

Dawn comes into mediation session saying mediation will probably not work. Her husband, Skip, treats her disrespectfully and it's very hard to be in the same room. She's also concerned because they still live together and she can't be in the same house with him anymore.

Skip says that the problem is that Dawn is sleeping with a guy that used to be his friend. If she would just stop doing that, then they could work on their relationship. He doesn't want the divorce.

They have two children, Gabby, age 4, and Jesse, age 6.

Instructions for Mediator:

Start the session by structuring the process:

- Explain your role as in charge of guiding the process
- Explain their role as making proposals and decisions
- Explain that process is not guaranteed, but often succeeds even when parties upset
- Explain how the session will be structured:
  - Focus is on the future and decisions about the future
  - Teach them how to make proposals
  - Teach them how to respond to proposals
- Ask for their initial thoughts and questions about decisions they need to make
- Help them make an agenda; have them decision first two topics; who goes first

Throughout mediation give lots of encouragement and education. Remind them to make proposals when they slip into criticisms. Reinforce small successes. Offer 3 alternatives if needed.

Try to get a complete agreement on their issues.

Instructions for Dawn:

You want to get out of the marriage as quickly and smoothly as possible. You won't say you are or aren't sleeping with his friend – say that who you spend time with is none of his business. And say that you don't have a "boyfriend."

You want to get agreements on a regular parenting schedule, so you can stop being in the house when it's his time with the children. You know he has been caring for the children as much as 60% of the time (because he doesn't work full time), but you think he should have no more than 33% of the time, because he has a short temper and drinks too much sometimes. At most, you'll settle for a 50-50 schedule on paper, because you know he'll get called to work and miss some of it. You have a regular work schedule, but his schedule is sporadic with special construction projects that prevent him from being with the kids on short notice. He works 1-3 days a week, usually on Thursdays through Mondays.

You want to keep the house in the divorce, which has equity of $100,000. You have a retirement savings account with $80,000 that you're willing to give entirely to him in exchange for the house.

You make more than he does and don't want to pay him any child support, because you think he could work more but doesn't try to get the hours. You can make progress on all issues, except don't agree to any child support. He doesn't deserve it because he's lazy.

From time to time, make criticisms of him for not working more and for being disrespectful toward you. But you also want to make progress to get the divorce over with.

Instructions for Skip:

You are angry about her wanting to get divorced, you are angry about her sleeping with your friend, and you are angry that she doesn't want you to be the primary parent of the children – even though you have been caring for them about 60% of the time because you work part-time and she works full-time. Be willing to settle for 50-50, but nothing less.

You make frequent comments about her new boyfriend and how you absolutely don't want him around the children.

You don't care if she gets the house in the divorce, as you're quite handy and can fix up a new house, if you have enough money to start with. The equity in the house is $100,000. The money she has in her retirement is $80,000, which is just enough for you to pay the down payment on a house you've been looking at – and you are very handy with home remodeling and repairs. But you want to stay in the current house as long as possible, so you can convince her to stay married. You say you'll need more money than just her retirement.

Say you want $1000 per month in child support to help you afford a new house. Say you found out from a lawyer that's what child support should be in your case. If she doesn't want to give you child support, say that she can't afford to get divorced and should try working on the marriage. Make progress, but don't agree to anything less than $500 per month in child support. She owes it to you after what she's done, and besides this economy has really hurt the availability of construction work in your area.

Interrupt a lot and explain that you are hyperactive and can't stop yourself. And you have the right to be angry about her sleeping with what-used-to-be your friend.

Divorce Mediation: Jeffrey and Kiran - Finances and Relocation

Problem Scenario:

Jeffrey and Kiran are both 32 years old. They have two children, Tracy, age 8, and Johnny, age 6.

Kiran comes to mediation saying it will probably not work. Her husband, Jeffrey, is insecure, depressed and angry about the divorce. Her main issue is that she wants to move out of Detroit and back to Grand Rapids, three hours away by car, where her parents live and an old boyfriend she has been in touch with recently. She wants the children to move with her, as she was the primary care-giver until the past two years. Kiran moved out a month ago to stay with a girlfriend in Detroit. She has the children on the weekends.

Jeffrey says that the problem is that Kiran has had a high-stress job working long hours in a law firm for two years and has drifted away from him. He doesn't want the divorce. He has been the primary care-giver for the children for the past two years. He is a school teacher and gets out at 3pm and picks up the kids. He says she needs to get away from her job, not him and not Detroit.

Kiran makes $120,000 per year and Jeffrey makes $60,000 per year. He says he'll be asking for child support and spousal maintenance. They own a small house worth approximately $300,000. Jeffrey doesn't want to move. They have no savings, but Kiran has a retirement account of $100,000.

Kiran is concerned that Jeffrey might be into internet porn, and might allow the kids to see it. Jeffrey denies that he's into internet porn.

Jeffrey is concerned that Kiran is having an emotional affair with her old boyfriend, Jimmy, who lives in Grand Rapids. Kiran denies this.

Malpractice Mediation – Dr. Jones and Attorney Hathaway

Problem Scenario:

Attorney Hathaway is a new lawyer who was hired to mediate a divorce between Dr. Jones and Mr. Jones. However, Mr. Jones stormed out of the first mediation session after only an hour and stated that he was going to take Dr. Jones to court for substantial alimony and child support. Attorney Hathaway and Dr. Jones had a long tearful talk after Mr. Jones left his office about how impulsive and abusive Mr. Jones was to Dr. Jones. Dr. Jones asked Attorney Hathaway to represent her at court, since the mediation was clearly over. Attorney Hathaway felt bad for Dr. Jones and decided that he was in the best position to represent her, because he'd gotten to know her so well and she was so vulnerable. He figured that only one hour of mediation should not be allowed to block him from protecting Dr. Jones from Mr. Jones in court. So, he took the case.

Needless to say, the case went badly at court for Dr. Jones and she was ordered to pay Mr. Jones substantial alimony and child support. The judge even agreed with Mr. Jones that Attorney Hathaway should not have taken the case since he had been their mediator, even though it had only been one hour. Attorney Hathaway had put in a lot of extra work—well above the retainer—and he sent Dr. Jones a bill for $10,000. Dr. Jones responded by suing him for malpractice in the amount of $100,000. They are required to attend at least one mediation session before going to trial on these two claims and they have selected you to be their mediator.

Please note that Attorney Hathaway can be quite arrogant and belligerent, insisting that he should be paid for all of his extra work and that he did nothing wrong (plus he needs the money). In fact, he believes he can prove that she would have received the same court orders or worse if someone else had taken her case, so there was no damage done.

On the other hand, Dr. Jones has frequent mood swings and frequent tears, and is really angry that she has gone from an abusive husband to an abusive lawyer and demands that she be compensated. She has gone on leave from her job as a pediatrician for a local community clinic because she is so distraught.

This is based on a real case. This is also a good case for discussing mediation ethics.

Large Group Facilitation: Derek the Disruptor

Derek has decided to join a planning committee for a volunteer group that is planning an annual conference and fundraiser. The committee meetings are open to any member of the group. He arrives late for the meeting, momentarily distracting everyone as he is carrying a stack of papers that he is barely able to hold under his arm. People make room for him to sit at the long table with a dozen other people attending.

Carrie is running the meeting. "As I was saying, the next item on the Agenda is to decide who is going to be in charge of publicity for the annual event. Who of you would like to volunteer for this subcommittee?" Three people raise their hands, including Derek.

Derek says: "Before we go any further, I think that we need to discuss the budget for this committee. I mean, how do we know what we can do without knowing the budget?"

Carrie says: "That is going to be one of the first tasks of the committee: figuring out what the various forms of publicity cost so that we can consider several choices at our next meeting. Right, Bonnie?"

Bonnie: "That's right. As chair of the subcommittee, I will be raising that at our meetings."

Derek: "But wait a minute! That's backwards. We need to simply decide on a budget, so that the subcommittee knows what it has to work with. Can't you see that?"

Carrie: "Derek, that's already been decided. We decided that before you arrived. Now, let's go to our next topic on the Agenda."

Derek: "But that's ridiculous. Carrie, you obviously are too young to know how budgets need to be developed first." Derek turns to Sam, the other person who raised his hand to be on the Publicity subcommittee. "Sam, you look like a successful businessman. Tell them how important it is to develop the budget first."

Sam: "Well, uh, there's different ways that you can do it. Some groups do it first, and some check out the current costs of various forms of publicity and then decide on their budget."

What can Carrie do or say to retain control of the large group meeting? (This example is discussed in Chapter 17.)

Detailed Table of Contents

Notes

1   American Psychiatric Association: Diagnostic and Statistical Manual of Mental Disorders, Fifth Edition. Arlington, VA, American Psychiatric Association, 2013, 645.

2   Allan N. Schore, *Right Brain Psychotherapy.* New York: W. W. Norton & Company. 2019, 220.

3   Ibid.

4   Martin H. Teicher, Scars That Won't Heal: The Neurobiology of Child Abuse. *Scientific American,* 286 (3), (2002): 68-75, 72.

5   Daniel Goleman, *Social Intelligence: The New Science of Human Relationships.* New York: Bantam Books. 2006.

6   Marco Iacoboni, *Mirroring People: The New Science of How We Connect with Others.* New York: Farrar, Straus and Giroux. 2008.

7   Rita Carter, *The Human Brain Book: An Illustrated Guide to Its Structure, Function, and Disorders.* London, Great Britain: Dorling Kindersley. 2009, 43.

8   Stephen W. Porges, *The Pocket Guide to The Polyvagal Theory: The Transformative Power of Feeling Safe.* New York: W. W. Norton & Company. 2017.

9   Id., at 45.

10 Michael Muskal, "Phoenix Lawyer Shot After Mediation Session Dies," *Los Angeles Times,* February 1, 2013.

11 "California Attorney Guidelines of Civility and Professionalism," *The State Bar of California,* Adopted by the Board of Governors on July 20, 2007, quoting excerpts from Section 13 and Section 19.

12 A. Holtzworth-Munroe, C. J. A. Beck, and A. G. Applegate, "The Mediator's Assessment of Safety Issues and Concerns (MASIC): A screening interview for intimate partner violence and abuse available in the public domain," *Family Court Review,* Vol. 48 No. 4, (2010): 646-662.

13 A. Holtzworth-Munroe, C. J. Beck, A. G. Applegate, J. M. Adams, F. S. Rossi, L. J. Jiang, C. S. Tomlinson, and D. F. Hale, D. F. (2021). "Intimate partner violence (IPV) and family dispute resolution: A randomized controlled trial comparing shuttle mediation, videoconferencing mediation, and litigation." *Psychology, Public Policy, and Law, 27, no.* 1 (2021): 45–64. https://doi.org/10.1037/law0000278

14 Robert A. Baruch Bush and Joseph P. Folger, *The Promise of Mediation: Responding to Conflict Through Empowerment and Recognition.* San Francisco, CA: Jossey-Bass. 1994.

15 Robert A. Baruch Bush, "Handling Workplace Conflict: Why Transformative Mediation," *Hofstra Labor & Employment Law Journal,* 18, no. 2 (Spring 2001), 367.

16 Tom Sebok and Lisa Neale, "When Supervisors Refer Employees for Mediation or 'Can You Take This Mess Off My Hands?'" *THE INDEPENDENT VOICE of the International Ombudsman Association,* Volume IV, Issue 2, August, 2009.

17 Bill Eddy and L. Georgi DiStefano, *It's All Your Fault at Work: Managing Narcissists and Other High Conflict People.* Scottsdale, AZ: Unhooked Books. 2015, 35-38.

18 Holtzworth-Munroe, 2021, 45.

19 This Respectful Meeting Policy and related tips first appeared in an article by Bill Eddy and L. Georgi DiStefano, "A Respectful Meeting Policy," *High Conflict Institute Newsletter,* April 2017.

20 Bill Eddy, *BIFF: Quick Responses to High-Conflict People, Their Personal Attacks, Hostile Email and Social Media Meltdowns.* Scottsdale, AZ: Unhooked Books. 2014, 110-112.

Acknowledgements

Bill Eddy

To my father, Roland, for teaching me to analyze problems; my mother, Margaret, for teaching me to understand people, not judge them; and to my stepmother, Helen, for teaching me service to others. Michael, you have been a like-minded and calm colleague over the past dozen years—it's been a joy to develop these ideas with you. I thank you, Megan Hunter, co-founder and CEO of High Conflict Institute and publisher of Unhooked Books, for being a steady business partner, creative colleague, skillful trainer, and co-author in this high conflict work for the past 15 years. A big thank you to the trainers and staff of High Conflict Institute for trying out and giving feedback on the principles and techniques in this book over the years, especially Louise Vandenbosch, L. Georgi DiStefano, John Edwards, Shawn Skillin, Michelle Jensen, Andrea LaRochelle, Trissan Dicomes, Susie Rayner, Betsy Johnson, Sarah Driver, and Jennifer Kustudia..

I would like to acknowledge my colleagues at National Conflict Resolution Center, who gave me a home base to start my mediation career in earnest nearly forty years ago and continuing up to 2019, including Barbara Filner, Lisa Maxwell, Robin Seigle, Kathy Purcell, Susan Finlay, Kim Werner, Joshua Hernandez, Steve Dinkin, Ashley Virtue, and many others. My early mentor, Woody Mosten, taught me so much and opened early opportunities for me to teach others. My colleagues with the Academy of Professional Family Mediators have given me the chance to know and work with the many of the founders of the professional family mediation field, including Don Saposnek, Chip Rose, John Fiske, Ken Neumann, Rod Wells, Steve Abel, Marilyn McKnight, Steve Erickson, Hilary Linton, Bob Horwitz, Michael Aurit, and so many others.

For the past ten years, I have enjoyed the opportunity to teach a course that includes high conflict mediation skills to law students at the Straus Institute for Dispute Resolution at Pepperdine University School of Law. I wish to thank my colleagues and friends there, especially Stephanie Blondell, Shellee Warnes, Deborah Jasmine, and Tom Stipanowich, as well as all the students who make teaching so worthwhile. For even more years, I have had rewarding collaborations with mediation colleagues with the Southern California Mediation Association (SCMA), including Terri Breer, Debra Dupree, and Susan Guthrie.

I owe a special debt of gratitude to my ADR colleague and friend, Tania Sourdin, Dean of Newcastle Law School, who invited me to Australia in 2008 and has brought me back year after year to teach a course as a Conjoint Associate Professor there and at Monash University Law School. I especially appreciate the working relationships and friendships I have developed over the years in Australia with other mediators and trainers, especially Tess Brook, Shiv Martin, and Nicole Cullen.

There are numerous others I wish to thank for their contributions to my career in many forms of dispute resolution, including many other mediators, my interdisciplinary friends with the Association of Family and Conciliation Courts (Peter Salem and the gang), my lawyer colleagues, my therapist colleagues, and others who are too many to name here. Finally, I would like to acknowledge and thank all of my mediation clients who have shared their ups and downs, while teaching me what to do and what not to do. I have learned so much from all of you.

Michael Lomax

To my parents, Alan and Audrey, you have taught me that argument can provide a positive opportunity for growth and learning. Bill, thank you for your mentoring, generosity and friendship over the years and this incredible opportunity. To my conflict management colleagues Alison Paine, Carolyn Stenberg, Lori Hurst, Rachel De Jager, and Shelley John, I am grateful to work with such a dedicated and engaging group of professionals. I wish to pay a special thanks to three people who have played an important role throughout my career, Patricia Lane, Laurence Johnson, and Mary Mouat. You have been my supporters, mentors and advisers over the years, and I am truly grateful. I want to thank those other colleagues and friends who have helped me to refine my ideas and beliefs about the field of conflict resolution and given me the confidence to take risks. To Megan Hunter, who has always been a patient and positive motivator in completing this project. Lastly, to the clients, who have taught me a lot about myself along the way and to strive to approach my work with empathy, curiosity, and humility.

The Authors

Bill Eddy, LCSW, JD, is a lawyer, therapist, mediator, and the co-founder and Chief Innovation Officer of the High Conflict Institute. He was the Senior Family Mediator at the National Conflict Resolution Center for fifteen years, a Certified Family Law Specialist lawyer representing clients in family court for fifteen years, and a therapist for twelve years. He serves on the faculty of the Straus Institute for Dispute Resolution at the Pepperdine University School of Law in California and is a Conjoint Associate Professor with the University of Newcastle Law School in Australia. He has been a speaker and trainer throughout the United States and around the world. He has written more than twenty books, including two award winners, and has a popular blog with Psychology Today with over 5 million views. Bill lives in San Diego, California with his wife.

Michael Lomax, JD is a lawyer by profession, mediator, and an international speaker/trainer. He practiced family law for over 20 years and early in his career, ceased his court practice to focus on mediation and collaborative law. Michael has conducted hundreds of mediations including family, workplace, multi-party, and court related matters. He has significant experience leading the design and implementation of workplace conflict management programs for large organizations. Michael has developed training for government, law firms, corporations, military, law enforcement, human resources, and unions. He has been an Associate Speaker/Trainer with High Conflict Institute since 2011 and lives on Vancouver Island.

CPSIA information can be obtained
at www.ICGtesting.com
Printed in the USA
LVHW080113130722
722916LV00007B/5